10/6 NET

MEDITERRANEAN
DEAD SEA
Mt NEBO
Mts OF ABARIM
Dibo
Arnon
Gaza
Hebron
Arad
Beersheba
Hormah
Raphia
Route by the coast
Route of the spies
Ije-abarim
Bene-jaakan
Moseroth
Mt Hor
Hashmonah
Kadesh
Punon
Rameses
Succoth
Caravan Route
Etham
Desert of PARAN
EDOM
Pi-Hahiroth
Migdol
Baal-zephon
Makheloth
Serpent of brass
Rissah
Desert of SHUR
Ezion-geber
Rimmon-perez
Marah
Rithmah
Wadi Gharandel
Elim
Desert of SIN
RED SEA
Dophkah
Hazeroth
Kibroth-hattavah
Rephidim
Mt SINAI (HOREB)
Miles
0 25 50 75

Men of Wisdom

MOSES

AND THE VOCATION OF THE JEWISH PEOPLE

ANDRÉ NEHER

Translated by

IRENE MARINOFF

NEW YORK
HARPER TORCHBOOKS

LONDON
LONGMANS

CONTENTS

Moses addressing the Jews and investing Joshua
(Haggadah of Serajevo, 13th cent.)

What is Moses to Us?

To assess the significance Moses has for the present time is no easy task. Of course there are cultural affinities. In the Pantheon of human achievement his name ranks among the first. Every list of great men is headed by him and the man in the street remembers him for his chronological priority. He is the *doyen* of all founders of religions, legislators, moralists, even of conquerors. The names of Zoroaster, Jesus, Muhammad; of Solon, Justinian, Robespierre; of Socrates, Confucius, Rousseau; of Alexander, Cæsar, Genghis Khan, are always second to his. The pageant of the heroes of humanity begins with Moses.

Moreover, a long artistic tradition, in sculpture and music, as well as literature, has made Moses the subject of innumerable works of art. Again and again his name, his personality, the problems connected with him have been put before the minds of educated men. Even an incomplete bibliography of literary works devoted to Moses or an abbreviated catalogue of artistic representations of him would fill volumes. He is the centre of a whole world of artistic forms, ideas and symbols.

Does this ubiquity of Moses and our instinctive attempts to give him a definite place in our cultural universe mean that we have any real relationship to him? Here we must beware of generalizations. The very fact that we can find Moses everywhere proves that we have really not found him at all.

Even a little learning will do to explode the myth that Moses stands at the head of any list of great men, and to relegate him to a more modest place in a monotonous catalogue. Before his day Neferrohu was a prophet, Hammurabi a legislator, Inotep a moralist, Sesostris a conqueror. As for the accumulated evidence provided by our general culture, this is treacherous and ambiguous. It evokes contempt rather than real understanding. It is true that millions of men picture Moses in the likeness given

Moses
(Fresco in the Synagogue of Dura-Europos, 3rd cent.)

Catacomb of Callistus (4th cent.)

Michelangelo (16th cent.)

him by Michelangelo. A certain number still admire him in the radiant silence and solitude in which Alfred de Vigny saw him. Others understand him by means of the symbol of the Tables of the Law, the emblems of justice and equity. But this does not prove that we have any real relationship to Moses. It simply shows that Moses is famous, and that men continue to try to find in him a confirmation of their own individuality, as they would do with other famous men. It was not the spirit of Moses that Michelangelo chiselled in marble. It was the spirit of humanism. This noble and robust pride, this serene and confident vitality, this mixture of force and tranquillity most certainly reflect the spirit of the Renaissance. But Moses only provides the mask and the name. Perhaps the unknown artist of Chartres Cathedral was right, and the face of Moses was long, emaciated, perplexed and full of pain? Or the artist of Doura-Europos, whose delicate, almost beardless Moses is radiant in his wonder

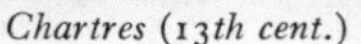

Chartres (13th cent.)

Dresden figurine (18th cent.)

and untried youth? Beside Alfred de Vigny's solitary, taciturn Moses there is Schiller's inventor and man of action. The Moses of Siegmund Freud harbours terrible complexes and compulsions. Churchill's Moses is a brilliantly dashing, gifted dictator and conqueror. Rossini, Darius Milhaud, Arnold Schönberg, Maurice Lévy have, by the magic of their music, conjured up the Moses of the librettist.

Our civilization contains in its storehouse of familiar symbols the famous Tables of the Law, which make Moses a popular figure even on the façades of our Law Courts. But it may well be that these upright tablets mark our progress rather in the spirit of Rousseau and Robespierre than in that of Moses himself.

Did not perhaps Nietzsche, with his symbolic broken and then restored tablets, understand the spirit of Moses better? For the

The French Revolutionary Code of Laws.

great legislator certainly held the Tables of the Law in his arm, but he also broke them one day at the foot of Sinai. Is the righteousness of Moses really the tranquillity of the established order? Or does it not rather resemble the wrath to come?

It is obvious that any relationship with Moses on the cultural level only tends to hide the real person by reducing it to conventional clichés. The best example of this distortion is those

Moses breaking the Tables of the Law (Il Parmigiano)

horns he is invariably decked with in both Christian and secular art. A mistake due to a translator's error on the part of St Jerome has now for more than a thousand years given the features of Moses a satanic cast. All this conceals the real Moses. His face is veiled. The veil must be lifted.

Can we get any help from the Bible? When all is said and done, our real link with Moses is the Bible, a book which, since

its beginnings more than 3,000 years ago, has not ceased to nourish and stimulate human thought, and will continue to do so. Though it may be for very different and even contradictory reasons, by our faith as well as our doubts, by our mysticism as well as our realism, by our prayers and our revolt, by our refusal as by our acceptance we are all disciples of Moses. Jew and Christian, Muhammadan and humanist, social reformer and dialectical materialist, even the existentialist philosopher—all acknowledge the Bible as the source or at least the foreshadowing of their creed. The mental outlook of modern man with all its paradoxes proves beyond doubt that Moses is still a force to be reckoned with.

Yet even this proof must, for serious reasons, be regarded with caution. As in the case of the evidence drawn from cultural considerations there is something ambiguous and artificial about the very fact that it is so general. What western attitudes of mind tend to retain is the myth of Moses rather than the reality. This must be exploded, and then the attempt must be made to show the real significance Moses has for the present time.

Even the most superficial examination will testify to the mythical proportions Moses has acquired today in the minds of the majority of those who believe in the Bible or base their arguments on it. It is true that wherever Biblical inspiration prevails, in monotheistic theologies and liturgies as well as in socialist doctrines, wherever the idea of temporal or spiritual salvation has a meaning, the part Moses plays is indeed impressive. In addition to literary and artistic monuments we find remarkable studies showing the place Moses occupies in the New Testament, in patrology, in Christian homilies, in the Qur'an and in the hadith, in medieval mysticism, and in the social utopias of the eighteenth and nineteenth centuries. Consequently the impression is gained that Moses has somehow entered into the spirit of the Christian, the Muhammadan, and the revolutionary.

Even here his personality is veiled, or rather, and this is worse, touched up or watered down. It is never the real Moses. In a religious context he is considered as a type. In a profane one as a point of reference. Moses belongs to the beginnings, hence to the past. There is no sign of Moses whenever we meet the challenge of the Bible or of reality. For the men of the twentieth century the access to Moses is blocked. For the Christian he is hidden by Jesus; for the Muhammadan by Muhammad; for the socialist by Isaiah, Rousseau, Shaw and Marx; for the existentialist by Job and Pascal.

This statement is more significant and entails more serious consequences than might appear at first sight. We must endeavour to see things clearly, and reduce those terms which are used so lightly, to their original meaning. Then we shall realize that saying one is faithful to Moses simply because one is faithful to the Bible, is a careless if not treacherous way of speaking. For Moses is not responsible for the whole Bible, but only for the Pentateuch—the Torah, the Law. Now this Law has not been absorbed by or integrated into the substance of the Bible

The death of Moses according to a Moslem MS. (14*th cent.*)

of Jesus, or Muhammad, or Karl Marx, or Kierkegaard. More has been rejected than accepted. The actual reality can rather be expressed by such antithetical formulae such as faith and law; dynamic and static morality; metamoral and reasonable service—which reveal the great differences between Moses on the one hand, and Christianity, Islam, positivism and existentialism on the other—than by other less expressive formulae showing their similarities. When Marcion in the early days and Simone Weil in our time express their rejection of Moses in violent terms, they are more sincere and more outspoken and in a certain sense more instructive than those who accept him uncritically. They help us to recognize the outlines of this Biblical figure which have been blurred by lack of discrimination.

It almost seems as though the name of Moses were the more frequently invoked the less men are prepared to obey his words. Here the myth of Moses comes in useful. It provides for the 'follower of the Bible' the illusion of adhering at least nominally to a doctrine which he has, as a matter of fact, rejected. The typical example of this is Judaism itself in spite of its tenacious fidelity to the Law of Moses. Yet even nineteenth-century liberal Judaism severed its connection with the Torah. Enlightened, emancipated and assimilated Jews considered the Prophets, the Psalms and the Wisdom books—in short everything that had been accepted by modern Christian or secular thought—as the only valid and valuable parts of the Bible, and this to the exclusion of the Pentateuch of Moses: the contemporary world had relegated this to the realm of archaic legends or primitive anachronism. Yet these very same Jews coined a new term, a new idea, 'Mosaist', and they themselves assumed this designation. Never before in the history of mankind had any religious denomination constituted itself with direct reference to the name of Moses. This nineteenth-century Jewish innovation is significant. At the very moment when the total disregard of the Law of Moses had reached its climax and constituted a scandal, because until then the loyalty of the Jews to the Law had been above reproach, the name of Moses was chosen to

la Philosophie admirés les effets | Dans son Temple aujourd'hui trouve un azile.
Sainte Liberté l'Egalité tranquille | Et déja l'Univers joüit de leurs bienfaits.

The Ten Commandments for general use (engraving by Callot)

conceal the treason. By becoming 'Mosaists' they actually renounced their Jewish individuality as children of Israel, and lost it in the crowd of those whose lip service to Moses was all the more superficial as they had long since ceased to observe his laws. By becoming 'Mosaists' the Jews began to share in that spiritual anonymity so characteristic of modern men who invoke the name of Moses but evade his message.

We must, then, in order to pass beyond the myth of Moses and find the real relationship between him and the present, modify the terms of the question asked at the beginning, not inquiring into the relationship between the Bible and the present, but between the Torah, the Law and the present.

Today, by way of a reaction to the development leading from the Renaissance to the beginning of this century, a rehabilitation of the Law is taking place, which at times assumes dramatic proportions. For the value of a thing we desire is always higher than the value of a thing we possess. Bialik and Kafka, who in different ways express the fundamental unrest of our age, are almost nostalgically obsessed by the problem of the Law. They felt the absence of the Law in their lives as their own sin and failure as well as that of their whole generation. They called for the Law, because it was torture and frustration to them to have been forced to deny it. Concluding an analysis of the spiritual crisis at the beginning of the twentieth century, Bialik cries out:

'Forge us the Law!' And on 19 October 1921 Kafka writes in his diary: 'It is not laziness, bad will, clumsiness . . . that cause me to fail, or not even fail in everything: in my family life, my friendships, my marriage, my profession, in literature, it is the lack of the soil, the air, the Law. It is my task to create them for myself. . . .'

Appeals of this nature cause Moses suddenly to become one of our closest contemporaries. This is not because our memory conjures up his person, not because the Bible belongs to the conventional arsenal of our civilization, but because an encounter with Moses today would be fresh and unprejudiced. Moses without horns and without a veil, in fact the authentic Moses, reveals himself wherever the Law in itself is the central subject of a thinker or a programme, where it regulates a conscience or a life.

Economists discover in Moses a socialism which is quite new and far better adapted to the needs of our age. Only yesterday the affinity between socialism and the Bible ranked as low as the

Origins of 'Mosaism': the law of Moses in Hebrew appears very decrepit. The modernized 'Law of Moses' is elaborated and granted by Napoleon.

poor do in the latter. Between the doctrinarians of the proletariat and the prophets of the Old Testament there existed a solidarity, which was more poetical than positive, more lyrical than active. It is true that the social thought of Blake, Hegel, Lamennais, Marx and Péguy was inspired by the spirit of 'the prophets'. But what they gave was rather an impetus than a programme, an inspiration rather than an implementation. Today people are more interested in the 'plan' of Moses, those social institutions the details of which he elaborated. These are striking in their boldness and efficiency. Moreover isolated experiments in communal living such as the kibbutzim of the Keren Kayemet (Jewish National Fund) in the State of Israel have introduced the ideas of Moses into the very structure of our most modern societies.

Religious thought is also drawing new strength from Moses. Today monotheism is no longer understood as a kind of vague and shapeless spirituality: it is now based on Moses, on his Torah, on the ritual laws of Leviticus, which are amplified and multiplied by the precepts of the Talmud. The views of Dr Henri Baruk, which differ so widely from those held by Jewish thinkers of the nineteenth century, are certainly open to dispute. Nevertheless they are a sign, found in the very concrete and almost objective fields of medicine and psychiatry, that a restatement of Jewish monotheism is in progress. This will have important repercussions among the other monotheistic religions. Formerly it was easy for any Christian, who was prepared to study the origins of his religion, to speak of a Judaeo-Christian tradition. In his mind he linked the prophetic elements in the Old Testament to the revelation of the New, leaving out Moses and his Law; that is, all types of 'Pharisaism'. Now a return to the origins (and is this return not characteristic of our age?) involves more precise and serious commitments. Moses and the Law as well as all 'Pharisaic' principles are recognized as being integral parts of Judaism. By putting a hyphen between Judaism and Christianity, and subsuming them under the same idea of 'monotheism', we implicitly admit that, in spite of their ineluctable differences, the Law and Faith, Pharisaism and

The world thirsts for the Torah
(*Engraving by Joseph Budko*, 1924)

Evangelism, Moses and St. Paul each have their immutable Biblical 'significance'. Recently Père Demann warned Christians that if they would be loyal to their monotheism, they must reconsider their attitude to Moses.

This re-thinking is all the more urgent, because Jewish religious philosophers for their part have already done so. It is no doubt true that certain Jewish thinkers have contented themselves with sharing the current religious ideas of our day and with the aid of a Berdyaev or a Saint-Exupéry they have rediscovered the fact that man has a ritual and cosmic vocation; on this basis they have gone further, to prove that Judaism has possessed these values since the days of Moses, and they were not even forgotten in the course of a century of rationalism. Martin Buber is a notable example. As Emmanuel Mounier writes, Buber's works represent 'the Jewish branch of existentialism', but it is a branch which draws its nourishment from existentialism rather than Judaism. However other Jewish thinkers, Jacob Gordin, Franz Rosenzweig and Abraham Heschel, make the Jewish tradition the starting point in their description of man and the universe. This tradition, they feel, has at all times, in all its manifestations and even in its present form, been rooted in an unswerving and fruitful loyalty to the Law of Moses.

It is not only the idea of the Law which allows us to pass from the myth of Moses to his reality. In recent years people have become very conscious of a serious and as yet unsolved problem; of an enigmatic and not assimilated presence in their midst; of something which they passed by, not in ignorance of its existence, but with indifference; until suddenly, one day, it was revealed as the most important thing of all. This problem, this something, is *The Jew*. The sudden promotion of the Jew to be the hero of the drama of our era has caused a quickening of interest in Moses, whose importance is reaffirmed by the times themselves.

When in 1945 morning dawned after the long and tragic night of the Third Reich, ten writers joined to draw up a provisional list of their shattered illusions and their hopes for the future.

Why ten? Because they were convinced that it was only under the sign of the Decalogue that the ruins of a world could be transformed into stones to build the future. The Law had been violated in its very foundations. It had to be restored to its very heights, so that the world could regain its balance. Each of the Ten Commandments concerns the whole of life in this world. So the ten writers took their turn to study the principles inherent in one of the commandments. It was obvious that the first word of the Decalogue, revealing the Presence of God beside man: 'I am the Lord, thy God', could best be illustrated by the life and thought of Moses, the architect of the whole Decalogue. Thus Moses as a person, and Moses with his symbol of the Tables of the Law, provided the foundation and the plan for a new and different world.

But why did Thomas Mann, who was chosen to write the portrait of Moses as the incarnation of the First Commandment, fail in his task? His Moses is ready-made, sugary, lacking in vitality. He resembles those prefabricated pictures of Moses which anyone can find in religious or secular libraries on the shelves devoted to theology or history. The reason for Thomas Mann's failure is, and there can be no doubt about it, that he approached his subject as a humanist. Deeply wounded as he was by the Nazi attack on the dignity of man, he endeavoured to recover at least some universal values by means of Moses. He discovered Moses *sub specie aeternitatis*. Now the need which had, perhaps, unconsciously led these writers to make their common survey did not belong to the order of eternity but to the order of the moment. Essentially the task, which each one of them had to recognize and formulate in explicit and ineradicable terms at a given moment in history, had nothing to do with man as an eternal type. It was concerned with man as an irreducible individual, held in the throes of a unique destiny: it was concerned with the Jew. It is true that the swastika had lacerated the whole of humanity; all the same its aggression centred on the Jew. Thus humanity could only be restored through a profound understanding of the position of the Jew.

This Jew, by Hermann Struck, c. 1920, asks heaven with anguish: What does the future hold in store?

If Thomas Mann had better understood the significance of his subject, he would have shown Moses as the man of the First Commandment, the man who is marked, sought out, and seized by God: 'I am *Thy* God.' Moses is the man who is destined to take second place, always in danger of being challenged; he is never alone with himself, for his solitude cannot but be an illusion or a mirage; and sooner or later he will meet his challenger in a kiss or a wound.

Thomas Mann would, then, have shown the reaction of Moses to this divine challenge: not as a call to himself as an individual, nor as an invitation to the whole of mankind, but as the Word, addressed once and for all time to the Jewish people. In future there will be no escape for this people. To be like the others? When God is the Other, the intimate Partner, the Thou? God is for ever meeting you. He is your way and the One Who bars the way, at the same time shepherd and wolf, father and judge, a loving and a jealous spouse. Whether hidden or openly He accompanies you, and when you think you can escape Him you are running towards Him. Though you are separated from Me by an infinity, you are Mine.

It is only when we keep the significance of Moses in mind that we can fully understand the 'mystery' of Israel, which has been so solemnly asserted in our era. Neither Abraham, nor Hosea, nor Jeremiah have thought and lived the unique destiny of Israel with a conviction similar to that of Moses. When the Jews speak of Abraham, they say: our Father. When they speak of Moses, they say: our Teacher. This is already an important distinction, but less fundamental than the following: Abraham is the father of the peoples of the nations, while Moses is the master of *this* people. In Abraham the communion of all peoples is prefigured. In Moses, in the heart of the very same communion, the unique vocation of the Jewish people is realized.

Hosea and Jeremiah have found sublime words to celebrate the indissoluble union between God and Israel. Feeling the full weight of this union, Moses has a deeper sense of his own, indestructible attachment to Israel. He is the only one of all the men in the Bible for whom God offers to let Israel disappear and to begin history with another people. Moses refuses. In spite of the immense risks, he wishes to continue history with *this* people, and it is *this* people which will continue in history. What an absurd undertaking, contrary to the clarity of God and the realities of the situation! However, the decision of Moses is as obstinate as it is far-reaching. Today we recognize its immediate and unalterable consequences in the reassertion of the Jewish people, whose very existence seems contrary to reason and who do not fit into the ordinary scheme of things. . . .

To give only one example: the Zionist adventure is one of the most amazing events in modern times. Many of its features have their parallel in similar experiments and can be explained by the laws of logic. Liberia, China and India immediately come to mind. Nevertheless, Zionism shows an irrational element: its unswerving fidelity to Palestine. Everything was opposed to this choice: the political constellation, the economic situation, the urgent need to provide a stable home for millions of persecuted men and women. Notwithstanding, by rejecting all 'territorial' considerations, the State of Israel was founded on *this* land and not on another. This decision which holds the whole adventure together can only be explained by the lasting effect of the decision of Moses. On this unjustifiable fact rests the fundamental vindication of the State of Israel. And it is

Prisoners of Seti I (Karnak)

regrettable that the constitution of the State did not mention Moses explicitly. It is true that the prophets of the Bible are invoked; but the founders of Israel have succumbed to the illusion of universality. They, too, have replaced reality by a myth. It may well be that the Bible, taken as a whole and characterized by the vague word 'prophetical', does not endorse the claim of the Jewish people to the land of Abraham. Claudel and Massignon do not fail to point this out. The spiritual reality which is the basis of the Jewish right to Palestine is that of Moses. Misunderstandings are cleared away, when his name is pronounced with courage and conviction. Then the relationship between Israel and this land is revealed as an indefinable yet manifest value.

It is an important event when a nation acquires its independence. In the twentieth century the Jewish people have experienced an even more serious one, the whole tragedy connected with the single name of Auschwitz. The meaning of this event as well becomes clear through Moses.

The external likeness is startling. If the whole system of Hitler's concentration camps is narrowed down to the Jewish persecution, there is none other which shows so many analogies to it as that of Egypt during the time of Moses. Egyptian documentation and the testimony of the Bible, both of which are more than 3,000 years anterior to the Third Reich, serve to bring the events closer, and everything takes place as though history were repeating itself after an interval of three thousand years.

However, we must note a less external similarity. In his *The Firstborn*, Christopher Fry has drawn attention to it. Educated and protected as he was at the court of Pharaoh, Moses escaped the fate of the Hebrews. He might have continued a long time living like an Egyptian, like a Jew assimilated and privileged, to all appearances like other men. But suddenly his Jewish conscience strikes him, as the Bible says in a few trenchant words: 'When Moses was grown up, he went out unto his brethren' (Exod. 2: 11). A significant and shattering journey. In an atmosphere of filth, sweat and blood Moses recovers his

Jewishness. By such an experience Moses has become the most familiar friend of the twentieth-century Jew.

For like Moses, the twentieth-century Jew has lived in the illusion that he was *like the others*. Till Auschwitz. Then, in the filth, the sweat and the blood, he awoke to the realization of an irrevocably different destiny. In the martyrdom of the six million European Jews, the typical figure was not, as might have been expected, the martyr; that is, the Jew, who had been faithful to his Judaism from the cradle to the grave. He knew that this was not the first holocaust; he was following the pattern of a covenant which had its days of unutterable splendour, but also its fogs and its nights. The typical figure was the martyr in spite of himself, the alienated Jew, who faced death with astonished eyes, 'astonished that they understood so little'. For him the discovery of the Jewish position meant a rude awakening. It was the Jew towards whose escape from his destiny all things seemed to conspire: a long-standing assimilation of the customs of society, at times coupled with complete ignorance of his Jewish origins; the tolerance of a secular and humanitarian century: a strong desire to 'wipe out' the past, to be forgotten; then suddenly to be thrown back into a fate, which he desperately tried to explain, and which, though still obscure, was unavoidable. The evidence of this 'going out unto the brethren' is too voluminous and varied to be recorded here in full. Some of these conversions were voluntary, others forced. Some manifested themselves in a rediscovery of Jewish spiritual values. Others showed an inner regrouping of all the powers of the personality. Two examples must suffice to indicate a multitude of similar experiences. One is the 'Moses' of Siegmund Freud, which was written in 1930, when the cataclysm of the Third Reich was foreshadowed. The advent of Hitlerism reminds Freud that he is a Jew, a fact which had almost completely escaped him during his seventy years of existence, and which now, suddenly, assumes capital proportions. Henceforth he seeks a subject, the analysis of which will serve less to satisfy his desire of knowing others than to assuage his thirst for self-knowledge. The subject he chooses is Moses. It is of secondary

Ghetto

importance and by no means detracts from the interest of the book as documentary evidence that the exegetical foundations of the study are open to attack, and the analysis in the last resort leads to self-destruction. The fact remains that, at the heart-rending moment when he discovers his Jewish conscience, one of the most typical representatives of the uprooted Jewish intelligentsia has written a book on Moses.

The second example comes from a poem which Benjamin Fondane, the young Jewish philosopher who meditated on Rimbaud and Hegel, 'did not have time to finish', because from Drancy the convoy took him to Auschwitz:

'Tis to you that I speak, ye men of the antipodes.
I am speaking as a man to other men,
With the little left in me of Man,
With the small voice remaining in my throat.
My blood o'erspills the roads. Would that it,
Would that it did not cry for vengeance!
The bugles blow. The beasts are cornered.
Let me speak to you with the same words
We had of old in common:
There are few you might understand.

The day will surely come, when all our thirst is
Slaked, and we shall be beyond the land of memory.
Death will have completed the labours of hate.
I shall be a handful of nettles beneath your feet.
Then . . . Well . . . Know that I had a face like yours;
A mouth that prayed like yours. . . .

Like you I have read all the papers and books,
And I knew nothing about the world,
And nothing about Man,
Although I often said I knew.

And when death, death came, perhaps
I pretended to know what it was; but truly,
I can tell you at this hour,

'hose accused of the crime of existing! . . . From ghetto to concentration camp.
Extract from the Livre sans Nom, *'the Book without a Name', engraved by*
n anonymous artist who escaped from Auschwitz, Hungary, 1947)

It entered fully into my astonished eyes,
Astonished that they understood so little.
Did you understand more?

Yet no!
I was not a man like you.
You were not born on the road.
Nobody has thrown your little ones into the gutter,
Like little cats whose eyes are not yet open.
You have not wandered from town to town.
Hounded by the police;
You have not known the disaster at dawn,
The cattle trucks,
The bitter sobbing of humiliation—
Accused of a crime you did not commit—
The crime of existing—
You never changed your name or face
To rid yourself of the hue and cry . . .
A face they spat upon!

. . . When you examine this handful of nettles
Which was I in another century,
In a history which is lost to you,
Only remember that I was innocent;
And on that day like you, mortals,
I also had a face
Marked by anger, pity, joy,

Simply . . . the face of a Man.

The poem bears the title *Exodus*. No doubt the reference to Moses is intentional. But even if it were a chance resemblance, for our century the real personality of Moses is better portrayed by Fondane in his tortured preoccupation with the 'Otherness' of the Jew, than by the lofty serenity of Michelangelo.

The Historical Moses

For centuries the Torah has been available, majestic with its monumental columns of regular script written on venerable, heavy parchment. In the square, chiselled characters of Hebrew the original work of Moses is offered to the world in the five books of the Pentateuch. They contain his account of the *Genesis* of the world, God's covenant with Abraham, Isaac and Jacob; his own biography and activity in Egypt at the time of the *Exodus*; the Laws of *Leviticus* revealed on Sinai; *Numbers*, the story of the wanderings of the Hebrews led by Moses across the desert of the peninsula of Arabia; finally *Deuteronomy*, the last speech of Moses, and the description of his death on the threshold of the Promised Land of Canaan. Today this text has been translated into nearly one thousand languages, a record unattained by any other book. Down to the last shades of meaning, caught by the translator, it is unvarying. The Pentateuch of Moses is at the same time the foundation stone and the threshold to the Bible: the twenty-four canonical books of the Jewish Bible, and the forty-six canonical books of the Catholic Bible. These are upheld and organized by the Pentateuch, which provides the sole approach to them. We invite the reader to concentrate and meditate on these texts. There is no better way of studying Moses.

Not so long ago such an invitation might have sounded somewhat naïve. Scholars, who approached the problem from the scientific or historical angles, were not prepared to admit either the authenticity of Moses or the textual integrity of the Pentateuch. All was under suspicion, criticized, rejected. There is a straight line of thought leading from Spinoza to the beginning of the twentieth century, the most famous exponents of which are the French theologian Richard Simon; the physician to Louis XV, Jean Astruc; and Julius Wellhausen, the Marburg exegete and historian. Their theory culminates in the assertion that the Pentateuch is nothing but a collection of a score of documents of very divergent and often contradictory nature, which were assembled during several centuries. Their final editing is supposed to have taken place about one thousand years after the time when Moses was assumed to have lived. From henceforth the right approach to Moses was no longer through the hieratic parchment of the Synagogue. You were supposed to use one of those rainbow editions of the Tübingen Bible, in which each colour evokes another source, another epoch, another author, each with a different initial J, E, D, P, JE, etc.—a nomenclature which has become almost as famous as that of chemistry.

Very soon a reaction set in to such extreme forms of criticism. Supported and made bold by the testimony of archaeological excavations, by sociology, by the comparative history of religion and myths, by an entire new way of thinking, this reaction is today finding its voice: 'The contents of our Pentateuch are, in general, very much older than the date at which they were finally edited [wrote W. F. Albright (*The Archaeology of Palestine*, p. 224) in 1949]; new discoveries continue to confirm the historical accuracy or the literary antiquity of detail after detail in it. Even when it is necessary to assume later additions to the original nucleus of Mosaic tradition, these additions reflect the normal growth of ancient institutions and practices, or the effort made by later scribes to save as much as possible of extant traditions about Moses. It is, accordingly, sheer hyper-criticism to deny the substantially Mosaic character of the Pentateuchal tradition.' There are also very many authors who, while using the method of textual criticism, attribute to Moses important parts of the Pentateuch, sometimes even verbatim: the Decalogue (Rowley, Baron); the apodeictic laws (Alt). Most frequently accepted in their general trend are: the historical passages (E. Jacob), the co-existence of the priestly and the deuteronomic spirit (Dusseau).

However, we must beware of too facile compromises and of well-conceived but illusory agreements. We are warned by the recent experience of Martin Noth. This exegete finished his study of Biblical history, undertaken with the best critical apparatus at his disposal, by declaring that it is absurd to call the intervention of Moses an 'historical' fact (*Histoire d'Israel*, 1954)! It is a timely warning! Thus even today, when there are so many historical pointers towards Moses, when so many scholarly 'reconstructions' of Moses and his achievement appear 'probable', there remains a doubt. It is possible that these pointers and these probabilities are artificial. It is still possible to write a history of Israel in which nothing that the Bible attributes to Moses, neither his achievements nor his biography, can be assigned to him.

When all is said and done, the choice remains inevitable. It is certainly not a choice between reality and a legend; it is a choice between two realities. One is cold, rational and logical; the other warm, suggestive and inviting. One forces the 'numinous' into its own dimensions like a post enabling one to control lighting systematically and with mathematical precision. The other allows the instantaneous diffusion of the 'numinous' to penetrate into the most intimate depths of the heart. In a book of this nature which does not endeavour to trace a logical fact down to its origins and in its developments, but a spirituality in all its surprising ramifications which defy analysis, the author will be permitted to make a definite choice. Of late so many studies of Moses following the analytical method have appeared that this one will be excused if it attempts to grasp the phenomenon of 'Moses' in its totality. The very subject of the enquiry authorizes us to do this, as well as the consciousness that, faced with the Bible, every man is entitled to expose himself unblushingly to what Pascal has called 'the risk'. The Pentateuch, then, shall be our term of reference; the introduction to our enquiry, and its summary, however feeble in comparison with the original.

Without touching the text itself we shall, like the scrupulous scribes of former times, add some judicious, but indispensable glosses. Beside the data of the text itself we shall incorporate in this summary the evidence of the oral tradition of the Jews as well as certain legends taken from the apocrypha which blend harmoniously with the spirit of the Pentateuch. In the margins

B

we shall place historical and chronological data as signposts. For as yet no agreement has been reached between the different hypotheses, all of which are based on the evidence of the Pentateuch, of history, and archaeology. On both sides arguments are brought forward in quick succession. The discussion is not yet at an end. In the left column the chief dates of the earlier chronology are printed, according to which Moses lived in the fifteenth century B.C. In the right those of the later, which places Moses in the thirteenth century B.C.

The ancestors: Abraham and Isaac (Haggadah of Serajevo, Northern Spain, or Central France, 13th cent.)

Moses saved from the water (Haggadah of Serajevo)

Earlier Chronology

1536: Accession of Thutmos I.

1520: Political activity of Hatshepsut, daughter of Thutmos I. After the short reign of Thutmos II she marries Thutmos III, who is utterly eclipsed till 1483.

	Later Chronology
Moses, son of Amram, son of Kohath, son of Levi, son of Jacob, son of Isaac, son of Abraham the Hebrew.	
God promises Abraham that he shall become a great and mighty nation and possess the land of Canaan.	
Four centuries elapse before the fulfilment of the promise. During these four centuries the history of the Patriarchs unfolds.	
The fate of Joseph, son of Jacob, brings about the descent to Egypt. The tribe of the Hebrews is settled in Goshen, to the north-east of the Nile Delta.	
A century of peace, during which the tribe become a people.	
Accession of a new Egyptian dynasty: the beginning of the persecution of the Hebrews.	1313: Accession of Seti I.
Critical stage in the persecution: all male children are to be cast into the Nile.	
Birth of Moses: His father: Amram. His mother: Jochebed, daughter of Levi. His elder brother: Aaron. His elder sister: Miriam.	1305.
After being hidden for three months, Moses is put in an ark of bulrushes, and concealed by the riverside. He is discovered by a daughter of Pharaoh, Bithya, who gives him to Jochebed to be nursed, and adopts him as an adolescent. His name, chosen by Bithya, means in Hebrew: *I have rescued him from the water*, and in Egyptian: *My son*.	1292: Accession of Rameses II.

The Punt campaign (Somaliland), led by Hatshepsut. The temple of of Der-el-Bahri.

1483: Death of Hatshepsut. Thutmos III becomes sole ruler. Violent reaction against the partisans of Hatshepsut.

The burning bush (Haggadah of Serajevo)

Moses grows up at the court of Pharaoh.
He studies all the learning of Egypt. In the service of Pharaoh he wages a successful war against the Nubians.

First contact of Moses with his Hebrew brethren.
Moses is shaken by a real discovery. He kills an Egyptian who was smiting a Hebrew and hides him in the sand. The next day he reproaches a Hebrew for quarrelling with one of his brothers. The Hebrew retorts immediately, indicating that he knows of the murder. The murder is divulged, probably by denunciation. Pursued by the agents of of Pharaoh, Moses escapes.

The exile of Moses in Midian.
The half-nomad Midianites dwell in the south of the peninsula of Arabia in the steppes bordering on Mount Horeb. Moses saves the daughters of Jethro the priest from the brutality of the shepherds. Jethro receives him into his house, gives him his daughter, Zipporah, 'the bird', in marriage, and puts him in charge of his flocks. Two boys are born: Gershom, *for I am twice a sojourner in a strange land*, and Eliezer, *the God of my father helped me.*
Jethro, who is thirsting after God, knows the monotheistic tradition of Abraham. The levitical and Egyptian education Moses has received is complemented by the teaching of Jethro.

1448: Death of Thutmos III.
Accession of Amenophis II.

The plague of locusts (Haggadah of Serajevo)

Death of the Pharaoh who persecuted the Hebrews: towards the end of the exile of Moses.

1225: Death of Rameses II. Accession of Menephta.

Moses eighty years of age: the vision of the burning bush.
God reveals himself to Moses and gives him the task of delivering the Hebrew people. Moses hesitates. God forces him to accept.

Moses returns to Egypt.
He leaves his wife and children with Jethro. Aaron comes to meet him.

First steps in preparation of the Exodus: failure.
The Hebrews have confidence in the message of Moses, but Pharaoh employs delaying tactics and redoubles the oppression. The Hebrews despair again. In agony Moses has recourse to God. God renews his promise and tells Moses and Aaron to go back to Pharaoh.

The plagues and other signs.
Before Pharaoh, Moses and Aaron transform their rod into a serpent. Then follow nine plagues, which affect the whole of Egypt: blood, frogs, flies, wild beasts, pestilence, boils, hail, locusts, darkness. At the outset the magicians succeed in bringing about the same effects, but soon they recognize the hand of God. Each time Pharaoh is readier to give permission for the Exodus, but when

Preparations for the Exodus
(Haggadah of the Earl of Crawford, Spanish, 13th cent.)

The night of the Passover
(Haggadah of the Earl of Crawford)

the plague ceases, he hardens his heart. He cannot yield, and persists in his refusal.

The announcement of the Exodus.
At the beginning of the new spring moon, which in future will be the first month of the Hebrew calendar, God announces the Exodus. This will take place during the night of the full moon. The Hebrews prepare the Paschal lamb.

Last meeting between Moses and Pharaoh. Pharaoh forbids Moses under pain of death to come into his presence. Moses replies: 'I shall never see you again.'

The Exodus: The night of the fifteenth day of the first month. The night of the Passover. Loins girded, feet shod, staff in hand, the Hebrews eat the Paschal lamb with unleavened bread and bitter herbs. They do not leave their houses, the doorposts of which are sprinkled with the blood of the lamb. God strikes all the firstborn of Egypt, from the firstborn of Pharaoh to the firstborn of the prisoner, and all the deities of Egypt. It is the tenth and last plague. It is a terrible night for Egypt. The entire population, from Pharaoh to the man in the street, urges the Hebrews to go. The Hebrews leave Egypt on the morning of the fifteenth day of the first month. The Passover is instituted for all time.

The first stages of the journey: From Rameses to Succoth, from Succoth to Pi-Hahiroth on

The crossing of the Red Sea
(Haggadah of Serajevo)

the shores of the Red Sea. It is the long way to Canaan. God has chosen it in order to avoid the road along the coast, which the recent Philistine invasion has rendered dangerous. Again designedly God has ordered the children of Israel to encamp by the Red Sea. Awakening of the Egyptians. They regret that they have let the Hebrews depart and believe they will catch them easily in the desert, where they are supposed to have lost their way.

Safe crossing of the Red Sea: The Egyptians are engulfed in the waters, which had parted to let the Hebrews pass through. Canticle sung by Moses, Miriam and the whole people.

Between the Red Sea and Sinai:
The first murmurs of the people: The waters of Marah are bitter. Moses casts a tree into the waters and they are made sweet. Halt at the oasis of Elim. The provisions of bread brought from Egypt are exhausted: manna falls for the first time in the desert of Sin on the fifteenth day of the second month. For forty years it will be the normal food of the Hebrews. It is renewed every day except the Sabbath. By a miracle, the amount gathered is the same for each person. On the eve of the Sabbath the ration is doubled. At Rephidim water is lacking: Moses smites the rock and water gushes out. The Amalekites attack the Hebrews. Joshua, the disciple of Moses, wins a victory. Jethro arrives, bringing Moses his wife and sons. Jethro recog-

The Manna
(*Haggadah of Serajevo*)

nizes the true God and advises Moses to appoint judges to aid him in his task of governing the people. When they approach Sinai, the Israelites have a sound foundation of justice and peace, taught by the first convert.

At the beginning of the third month: *The revelation of the Decalogue on Mount Sinai.* Solemn appearance of God. God makes a covenant with His people. Moses stays on Sinai for forty days and nights without eating or drinking. God gives him the stone tables on which he has written the Decalogue. Revelation of the codes of civil, penal and religious law, and the commandments concerning the sanctuary.

The eve of Moses' return to the camp: *the people make a molten calf and worship it.* When Moses comes down again from Sinai next morning, he breaks the Tables of the Law. The idolators are chastised. Levites are chosen as priests.

Moses returns to Sinai: he prays God to pardon the people. Theophany of the rock. Revelation of the mercy of God. When Moses descends again from Mount Sinai his face is radiant. God grants forgiveness on the tenth day of the seventh month: institution of the solemn fast of Yom Kippur.

The Tent of Meeting is built: it is established on the first day of the first month of the second year. The two eldest sons of Aaron die on this day. The revelation of the laws of

The Tables of the Law
(Haggadah of Serajevo)

Leviticus concerning: sacrifices, dietary laws, purification, feasts, the sabbatical and the jubilee years. The celebration of the Passover on the fifteenth day of the first month: the first anniversary of the Exodus. Census of the people and organization of the camp.

On the twentieth day of the second month the camp is struck: *Israel leaves Sinai* in order to reach Canaan by way of Kadesh. There are several delays: the incidents at Taberah and Kibroth-hattaavah (murmurings quail), and the quarrel with Miriam, who is struck by leprosy and healed through the prayers of Moses.

Arrival at Kadesh-Barnea on the first day of the fourth month.

The dispatch of twelve spies.
After an absence of forty days they return and declare that the conquest of Canaan is an impossibility. Only Caleb and Joshua preach trust in the Lord. There is a general revolt. In their folly the people want to return to Egypt. Theophany. The guilty are punished. All men who were over twenty at the Exodus shall die in the desert. The younger generation shall wander there for forty years. A group of Hebrews try to force their way into Canaan: *the defeat at Hormah.*

Victory of Menephta?

Thirty-nine years of desert wanderings. The route lies towards the east arm of the Red Sea, through Arabia towards the Dead Sea.

Is there any connection between the tablets of Ras-Shamra and the sojourn of the Hebrews at Kadesh?

Last discourse of Moses (Haggadah of Serajevo)

Amenophis III.
Amenophis IV.
The El-Amarna Letters.
The beginning of the conflict in Canaan.

Prolonged stay at Kadesh and halts during the various stages of the journey.
Various episodes: the revolt of the Levite Korah and his men. Faint-heartedness of the people. The serpent of brass. Above all, a continuous revelation and amplification of the different parts of the *Torah*.

At the beginning of the fortieth year: the death of Miriam.
Contact with the kingdoms of Edom and Moab, which are passed on the way.

Death of Aaron.
The Moabites and Midianites endeavour to protect themselves from the Hebrews through the curse of *Balaam*, who is forced to bless Israel.

Conquest of Transjordan.
Contamination by the dissolute customs of the Moabites and Midianites: *Pinhas*, grandson of Aaron, saves the purity of Israel, Punishment of the Midianites.
On the first day of the eleventh month Moses begins his *last discourse*, which will be Deuteronomy. Joshua appointed as successor to Moses.
Moses commits the Book of the Torah to the Levites.
The Canticle of the destiny of Israel.
Last blessings.
Death of Moses on Mount Nebo on the seventh day of the twelfth month.

The peoples from the Sea disturb the equilibrium in Canaan.

It is true that at the birth of Moses the history of the Hebrews had entered a critical stage. This history is already four hundred years old and shows characteristic features, which Moses escapes for a time in his refuge at the Egyptian court, but which he will rediscover later. Ethnically speaking the Hebrews are Semites, kinsmen of the numerous nomad or semi-nomad tribes who wander across the vast lands of the Middle East, with Anatolia as their northern, the Tigris as their eastern, the Mediterranean as their western, and Egypt, Arabia and the Persian Gulf as their southern borders. The original clan lived in Sumeria, in the highly civilized city of Ur, which was situated in the most southern part of Mesopotamia. The victorious wars waged by Hammurabi against the Sumerians obliged the Hebrew clan to emigrate to the north, to Haran, between the Euphrates and the Tigris. There an important event takes place which divides the original clan into two parts. One remains in Haran and soon loses its identity among the neighbouring Arameans. The others become nomads again. They move to the south and reach the land of Canaan between Phoenicia and Egypt. This is the beginning of a mystical adventure, which is superimposed upon the normal life of the tribe. Externally they appear in Canaan as a group of shepherds, who are at times driven by famine or drought to seek pastures elsewhere, among the Philistines or even in Egypt. But in the soul of the tribe there dwells a hidden knowledge.

It is the knowledge of a God who is not like the other gods: He is One, Creator and Master of heaven and earth. His clearly expressed will blends with the ideal of justice and righteousness. His hidden will, which is communicated to men by prophetic visions, calls them to immediate or more distant tasks. At Haran, Abraham the Hebrew had the first of these visions. It was made known to him that he must be a just man, and at the same time that some day he would be the father of a great people, to whom the land of Canaan was promised, and who would walk together in the ways of charity and righteousness on that very land. This promise is realized in stages, though not without terrible and even tragic trials. The first son of Abraham, Ishmael, goes his own way. But Isaac, the child of his old age, follows the divine pattern. One of the two sons of Isaac, Esau, breaks away. But Jacob, the other, wins through in a famous night, when he wrestles with the Angel of the Lord, and receives the name of Israel ('the man who has striven with God') which his descendants will bear after him. The clan of Israel consisted of seventy souls, when they went down to Egypt, driven by an unusually great famine and also by the fact that one of the sons of Jacob, Joseph, had been sold to Egypt as a slave, where he had eventually become the vizier of Pharaoh. In Egypt the tribe becomes a people. The memory of the past fades. Were it not for circumcision, the sacred sign of the covenant made by God with their ancestor Abraham, the children of Israel would scarcely remember God, or their ancestor, or the promise, which had formerly upheld their tribe. And were it not for the Levites, the descendants of Levi, the third son of Jacob. They keep a jealous watch over the past and hand down to each other the knowledge of their religion and their vocation as a sacred trust. Moses is one of these Levites. But why are his parents obliged to throw him into the Nile at birth? The history of Egypt, which overlaps the story of the Bible, throws some light on this as well as on the later events of his life. However, we are now at the point of division of the two chronological tables, and, apparently, a choice must be made between the left- and the right-hand columns.

In the left column Moses was born in the fifteenth century before Christ. The scene, of which Moses becomes a part, is almost romantic. The anonymous Egyptian figures of the Pentateuch—Pharaoh, his daughter and his priests—become full of life and colour.

We are on the eve of the expulsion of the Hyksos. It is a spectacular and dramatic event, the force of which and its relationship with the story of the Bible have been analysed by Pierre Montet. The Hyksos are but one among many migrators from Asia to shake the old empires of the Middle East—Hatti, Sumeria, Elam, Phoenicia—at the end of the third and the beginning of the second millennium, causing political and cultural upheavals which resemble those of a later date connected with the Germanic tribes during the decline of the Roman Empire. But they were the only ones to penetrate deeply into Egypt, the oldest, most respected and most powerful empire of the day. They occupy the delta, the richest, most active, and most truly 'Egyptian' district in the Empire of the Nile. The Hyksos kings establish their court at Memphis, the capital of twelve Egyptian dynasties, beside the pyramids and the sphinx, relics and symbols of a civilization already a thousand years old. The Egyptian Pharaohs are forced to retreat up the Nile valley and enclose themselves at Thebes. Egypt is divided for a long time. Upper Egypt, which is only a corridor bordered by immense deserts, is held by the Egyptian Pharaohs. But Lower Egypt, the large delta, the granary, with its outlets on the Red Sea in the east and the Mediterranean in the north is, according to the most likely reckoning, held by the Hyksos for nearly two centuries, between 1750 and 1580.

The Hyksos are Semites. If the usual explanation of their name is correct, they were shepherds like the majority of the Semitic nomads of the second millennium. In Egypt the sociological law of assimilation works rapidly: the conqueror adopts the civilization of the vanquished. After two centuries of evolution the Hyksos settlers are no longer distinguishable from the

Semitic tribe seeking refuge in Egypt

Egyptians, whose customs, religious beliefs and forms of administration they have adopted. Yet in one thing they differ from the Egyptians. Unlike them, they are not isolationists. As Semites on African territory the Hyksos continue their neighbourly relations with the Semites of Canaan, Phoenicia and Mesopotamia. It is easy to imagine that Semite slaves were set free by the Hyksos Pharaohs and raised to the highest offices. Wandering Semitic tribes driven by famine may have reached the frontiers of Egypt and been hospitably received by the Hyksos. Within the framework of a Hyksos government, the story of Joseph and Jacob and the settlement of the family of Israel—all Semites—in the land of Goshen to the east of the delta, is easily explained. This very complicity between the Hyksos and their Hebrew vizier will compromise the Israelites when the Hyksos are driven out of Egypt; when, according to the Bible, 'there arose a new king over Egypt, which knew not Joseph' (Exod. 1: 8). It is implicit that he no longer wished to know him.

The war waged by the Theban Pharaohs against the Hyksos was long and bitter. The land had to be won back inch by inch. Middle Egypt was liberated by Kames; the delta by Ahmes, who pushed the siege against the Hyksos in Avaris, close to the eastern border, and pursued their defeated army as far as Canaan,

where their remains disappeared. Ahmes does not only begin a new dynasty, but a New Empire, ruled by three dynasties (the eighteenth, the nineteenth and the twentieth) and lasting for almost five centuries. This is the heyday of Egyptian power, the inception of which witnessed a violent outbreak of chauvinism. All evidence of Hyksos rule is traced and eliminated. Every sign of their presence—monuments, steles, sarcophagi, papyri—disappears beneath the blows of the hammer. The Egyptians succeeded so well in effacing their memory that we have not a single document concerning the two centuries of Hyksos rule in Egypt. The very foundations of the New Empire have been impregnated with the hated blood of the Asian mongrels. The shadow of the Hyksos weighs like a nightmare on liberated Egypt, and hatred of all Asiatics dominates the psychology of the Egyptian at the outset of the New Empire.

The change of attitude indicated by the verse of Scripture is an immediate consequence of the departure of the Hyksos. The tribe of Israel, which has by now developed sufficiently to constitute a people, has settled in the very province of Avaris where the last act of the drama took place. The Israelites did not follow the retreating Hyksos. As they remain, they become the object of a psychological transference. The psychosis of hatred chose them as victims and surrounds them with the myth of the seditious and sacrilegious Asiatic. The enslavement and the persecution of the Hebrews begins as a consequence of the expulsion of the Hyksos. They are part and parcel of the war the first Pharaohs of the New Empire waged against the Asiatic spectre.

The shape this enslavement took, which is so graphically described in the first pages of Exodus, is conditioned by two political factors: Egyptian imperialism and its corollary, economic power.

The first rulers of the eighteenth dynasty are indeed energetic conquerors. If Ahmes I and Amenophis I consolidate their power mainly in the south, penetrating deep into Nubia, their most illustrious successors, Thutmos I and Thutmos III, whose reigns take us down to 1450, lead Egyptian armies into Asia.

The royal wig: everything centres round Pharaoh

Thutmos I reaches the Euphrates and is astonished that its waters, unlike those of the Nile, flow south to reach the sea. Thutmos III follows his footsteps, crosses the Euphrates, and subdues the Mittanians, the most representative Asiatic people of the day. Canaan, Phoenicia, their ports and their hinterland, the vast regions of Naharina between the Mediterranean and Mesopotamia are tributaries of Egypt and acknowledge Pharaoh as 'King of the Universe'.

The Pharaohs of the eighteenth dynasty, like their predecessors of the Pyramid Age, leave grandiose monuments as a witness to their power. The Ahmeses and the Thutmoses are great builders: beneath the repairs made later by the sovereigns of the nineteenth dynasty, the grand scale of the original buildings can still be appreciated. The first plans of Deir-el-Bahari, of Luxor and Karnak were conceived by them. These buildings serve religious or secular ends; there are palaces and temples, but also

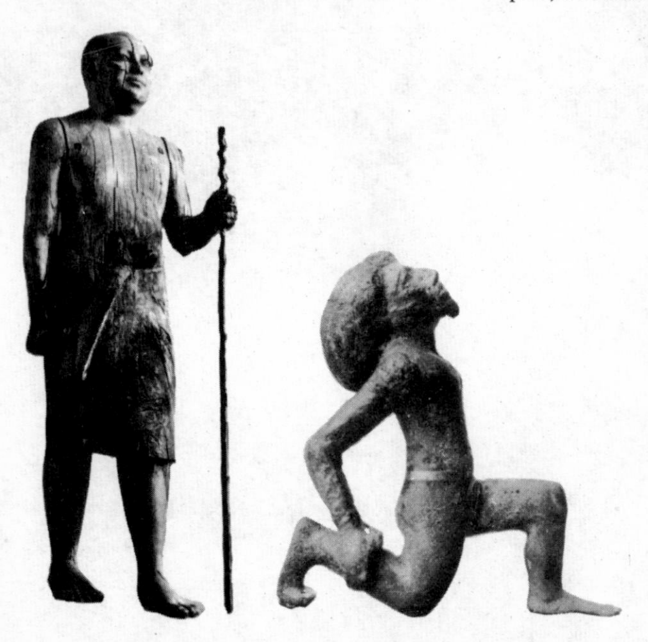

The administrator. His sceptre is the staff

The captive in chains between life and death

barracks, military depots and fortresses. For at the beginning of the New Empire the army appears as a new force by the side of the age-old traditional Egyptian forces: the priesthood and the civil administration. The building sites that spring up all over the country require labourers. The time has come when the political power of Egypt is doubled by her economic superiority. The Biblical account of the slave labour of the Hebrews, the making of bricks and the building of military depots, appears highly probable when seen in this framework.

It is a fascinating prospect: the historical setting of the eighteenth dynasty is not only capable of providing a general framework for the events related in the Bible. It may also account for certain details, particularly the astonishing fact that a daughter of Pharaoh saved a Hebrew boy, whom she later gave the name of Moses and adopted as her son.

This Egyptian princess, who defied the laws of her father and

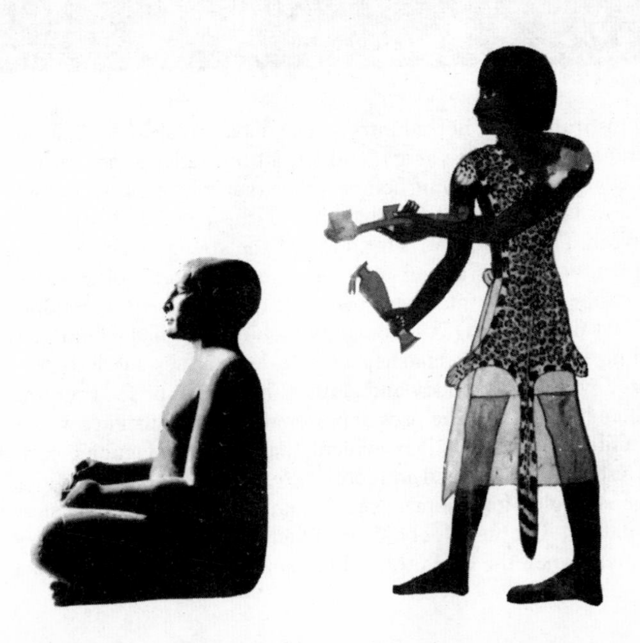

The scribe listens and writes down the cyphers and the mysteries

The priest interprets the sacred symbols

Hatshepsu

the institutions of her country, must have possessed a strong personality and great energy, and her authoritative action seems to belong to the realm of fiction rather than historical fact. Yet we find in the list of the Pharaohs of the eighteenth dynasty between Thutmos I and Thutmos III the strange woman-king, Hatshepsu. She is a king and not a queen: the ending *u* is a masculine one and must have been put there on purpose to hide the fact that this king is a woman, who but lately had a feminine ending to her name: Hatshepsu*t*. On her statues she is represented with a man's body and clothes: her feminine features are hidden by a beard. She rises to power after some intrigues which are still obscure. But it is evident that different factions, each representing an old and influential court or religious tradition, have struggled for the mastery. When she reached adolescence her father, Thutmos I, abdicates in her favour. This is the very moment when the daughter of Pharaoh can save and bring up a young Hebrew. Thutmos II marries her, but his reign is short. Then she becomes the wife of Thutmos III, whom she totally eclipses. For a long time he is no more than a prince consort. For the period of fifteen years Hatshepsu is the only Pharaoh. Moreover, as a daughter, a wife, and mother of a Thutmos, she is a great builder. And one is led to think that, as the Bible indicates, the saving of Moses was an isolated act, while the other Hebrews continued their forced labour. The magnificent temple of Deir-el-Bahari is the work of Hatshepsu. It is built in the south, in the direction of Punt (Somaliland), where Hatshepsu sent a memorable expedition. The paintings of Deir-el-Bahari have commemorated the details of this expedition, to which subsequent annals add great wars waged by the Amazon-Pharaoh against the Ethiopians. Now Alexandrian historians, though also of a later date, recount that Moses was educated by his adoptive mother as an Egyptian noble and won signal victories over Punt and Ethiopia. These fragments of tradition put together go to prove the identity between Hatshepsut and the

Temple of Deir-el Bahari

daughter of Pharaoh who saved Moses. In addition to this Thutmos III gives rein to his rancour once Hatshepsut is dead. As he could not touch the woman who had humiliated him during her lifetime, he destroys all traces of her and her name on the monuments and royal tablets. He persecutes her adherents and followers. Has the fifteenth verse of the second chapter of Exodus nothing to do with this political re-orientation? Moses, the protégé of Hatshepsut, no doubt like many others, is threatened with death and only owes his life to his flight from Egypt. Just as the Hebrews a century earlier had been victims of hatred for the Hyksos, now one of them, Moses, bears the consequences of hatred for Hatshepsut. As regards the enslavement of the Hebrews, this continues under Thutmos III. According to Biblical testimony several decades had to elapse and a new Pharaoh ascend the throne before the hour of liberation struck.

This new Pharaoh is Amenophis II. Does the agreement between the Bible and historical documents continue, and is it possible to place the Exodus with the same likelihood as the persecution during the reign of the eighteenth dynasty?

Actually there is nothing about Amenophis II which would make it likely that the Exodus took place during his reign; and the same is true of his successor, Thutmos IV, except that these brave and cruel warrior Pharaohs are now induced to come to terms with the Mittanians, who have raised their heads again, and to sign treaties and conclude marriages with them. These are signs of weakness in the Egyptian empire, which will increase in the years to come, but not in themselves sufficient to justify or explain the Exodus.

However, under the successors of Thutmos IV—Amenophis III and Amenophis IV—there is a striking parallelism between the Biblical narrative and historical events.

With these two Pharaohs we come to the age of El-Amarna, a half century of strange cultural and religious changes which will be explained presently. It was at the same time an age of political decadence, the echoes of which have come down to us in nearly four hundred tablets, which make up a regular archive of foreign policy. These were discovered towards the end of the last century at El-Amarna, half way between Thebes and Memphis, and they contain the diplomatic correspondence between the court of Egypt and its officials and subjects in Canaan. The whole correspondence is highly dramatic. In more and more pressing terms the Egyptian governors call for reinforcements. Their letters and reports are full of it. Their subjects in Canaan are getting out of hand; some are afraid, others are traitors. Unless Egypt strikes quickly, Canaan will fall to the enemy. Which enemy? First of all there are the Hittites, whose power is growing in the north. They are already masters of Anatolia, and are descending southwards. They have reached Phoenicia, and are threatening Canaan. Then there are the Arameans, a nomad tribe, wandering across the eastern desert and penetrating into the valleys. Finally there are the Habiru, of Semitic origin as well, who seem to follow a methodical plan of conquest. Systematically they attack the towns, destroy them, and only spare those who are willing to submit to their yoke. The letters break off at the very moment when Jerusalem announces that she cannot hold out any longer against the victorious Habiru.

The Habiru! It is a great temptation to identify them with the Hebrews. Etymologically speaking the obstacles are only slight. Although the military campaign described in the El-Amarna tablets do not completely coincide with those contained in the Book of Joshua in the Bible, many historians are prepared to identify the two, and this all the more so, as the excavations at Jericho (according to the Bible version the first city the Hebrews destroyed in Canaan) seem to prove that the walls were destroyed during the El-Amarna period. Even when we take the manifold objections into account—they are too numerous to be treated here and are met in very varying ways—and when we make allowances for the fact that many of the readings and the etymological identifications are hypothetical, a coherent story emerges. About half a century lies between the accession of Amenophis II and that of Amenophis III: 1450–1410. If the Exodus took place during the first years of Amenophis II, the capture of Jericho and the gradual penetration into Canaan took place during the first years of Amenophis III. J. Garstang, the famous excavator of Jericho, gives the precise dates of the forty years the Hebrews took to cross the desert according to the Biblical reckoning, as from 1447 to 1407! Furthermore the Bible narrates that the conquest took a long time, and that Joshua, the disciple of Moses, could scarcely complete it and had to leave the remaining operations to his successors, the Judges. Can we not find traces of this lengthy conquest (1407–c. 1350) in the letters of El-Amarna, which are contemporary to the reigns of Amenophis III and IV? If we adopt this argument, light is shed on every stage in the history of Moses, the main points being: the expulsion of the Hyksos (enslavement of the Hebrews in Egypt); the caprice of Hatshepsut (Moses is rescued from the Nile by the daughter of Pharaoh); the reprisals of Thutmos III (Moses is persecuted); the reign of Amenophis II (the Exodus); the reigns of Amenophis III and Amenophis IV (the death of Moses before the plain of Jericho and the conquest of Canaan by the Habiru—Hebrews).

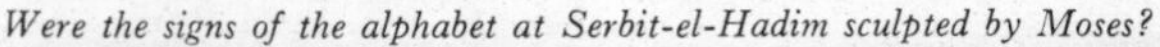

Were the signs of the alphabet at Serbit-el-Hadim sculpted by Moses?

Like iron filings in a magnetic field other documents and events in the history of the Middle East arrange themselves round these points of reference, and it is not erroneous to connect them with Moses. The inscriptions of Serbit-el-Hadim on Sinai date from the fifteenth century. That is the only thing known with any certainty about them. As for the rest, these hieratic signs have not yet been deciphered. There are some scholars, however, who would interpret them as the story of a rebel . . . none other than Moses, carving his hatred of Egypt in the rocks of Sinai with indelible letters! Others would recognize the first alphabet in them. Moses on Sinai as the inventor of the alphabet! The subject figures in the *Lives* of Alexandria and is still discussed by scholars. But, above all, it is the extraordinary spiritual adventure of Amenophis IV which is connected with that of Moses. Too many excellent studies have already been made of the work of Amenophis IV for it to be necessary to discuss it at any length. Everything about him is attractive: the poetical and exciting quality of his life; the simple beauty of

Ikhnaton and Nefretete, the romantic royal couple

the love his wife Nefretete bore him; the happy family life enjoyed by this couple, to which the plastic arts, so surprisingly revived during his reign, bear witness. Everything he does is done fully: his politics, his fanatical struggle against the priesthood of Amon, the patron deity of the dynasty, at Thebes; his search for a new capital, which shows him as an innovator; his religious reforms which spring from a passionate quest for unity. It is the unity of the good and the true, the unity of the opposing forces of nature in the one disc of the sun—the unity of life and death in the creative power of this disc—Aton, the supreme God, whose rays are the hands that bestow happiness. Amenophis becomes Ikhnaton, the son of Aton. His capital: the city of Aton, Ikhutaton (the El-Amarna of today). The hymn to Aton has the sober dignity and the touching eloquence of the Psalms. The historian, who has made a study of the human conscience in all its trends, affirms that with Ikhnaton it reaches a critical point in its development.[1] At least this is, outside Israel, the one moment in the whole of antiquity when monotheism is reached. It was a passing moment, as the immediate successor of Amenophis IV, Tut-Ank-Amon, who is more famous for his sarcophagus and his tomb than for his government, returns to conventional religion and restores the cult of Amon, whose name he bears, in all its rigidity. It is well nigh impossible to resist the temptation of seeing in the adventure of Amenophis-Ikhnaton a consequence of the lightning passage of Moses in Egypt, which took place a few years before. When all is said and done, the main value of the coincidences established in the left-hand column lies in the fact that it enables us not only to follow the repercussions of the history of Moses and the Hebrews step by step from their enslavement to the conquest of Canaan, but also to capture the spiritual echoes in Egypt of that religious storm, the Exodus.

The chronology of the thirteenth century on the right-hand margin is less full and more sober. The arguments in favour of it are neither brilliant nor romantic. They are the severe considerations of exegesis, textual criticism, archaeology. They may rest on the reading of a single word, the interpretation of a piece

[1] J. Pirenne, *Les grands courants de l'histoire universelle*, I, p. 65.

Which of these two Pharaohs saw Moses? Thutmos III or Rameses II?

The power of Rameses II; the columns of Karnak

of pottery. As a whole they may convince the serious historian, but hold no appeal for the uninitiated. Moreover the life of Moses itself is not, in its intimacy, linked with any outstanding event. It is a part of a greater whole: the life of the Hebrew people, which is itself abbreviated, and is presented in its general outline rather than in detail. The framework is rich. There are the vivid colours of the New Empire at the height of its power, the nineteenth dynasty, with its Rameses; the gigantic colonnades of Karnak, the obelisks of Luxor, the great alliance between the Egyptians and the Hittites, and the valley of the kings. In comparison the history of Israel appears rather dull and shadowy, lacking finesse and relief.

According to this reading we must suppose that the tribe of Jacob penetrated into Egypt under Amenophis II or Thutmos IV. This pharaoh comes to an agreement with the Mittanians

ISRAEL *inscribed in hieroglyphics on the stele of Menephta* and marries an Asian princess. It is the end of the anti-Asiatic psychosis, which was a consequence of the war against the Hyksos. Among other tribes to which Egypt has begun to open her gates, the Hebrews are received with kindness. The Habiru of El-Amarna are not to be identified with the Hebrews whom Moses led to the very gates of Canaan, since Moses was only born after the end of the El-Amarna period. The religious reforms of Amenophis IV owe nothing to Moses, because they are anterior to him. (Are they indebted to Joseph, whose double the vizier Yannamu, quoted in the El-Amarna letters, might be? It is a tentative question, not to be voiced too loud.) The persecution of the Hebrews began under Seti I and continued under the long reign of Rameses II (1292–1225). The Hebrews help to build the mighty Egyptian Empire. When it begins to crack under the successor of Rameses, Menephta; when it is battered by the blows of new hordes of invaders, the Men from the Sea, who are as dangerous as formerly were the Hyksos, the Hebrews succeed in escaping from Egypt. That is the Exodus of 1220. Thanks to the troubles in Canaan, owing to the activities of these Men of the Sea, some of whom are familiar under the name of Philistines, the Hebrews manage to settle in Canaan, though not without many set-backs. An engraved stele, erected by Menephta a little later, mentions Israel in a list of several conquered peoples. This is the first appearance of the name of Israel in archaeology and the sole definite connection between the Bible and Egypt. As a matter of fact it is this very appearance of the name of Israel on the stele of Menephta which might tip the balance in favour of the chronology of the thirteenth century. Yet even the reading of the name has been disputed (perhaps it ought to read 'Jezreel', which is a valley in Canaan); the context itself is obscure (it is not known whether a settled nation or a nomad tribe is meant); as on many other antique stelae, the king may have included in his list of

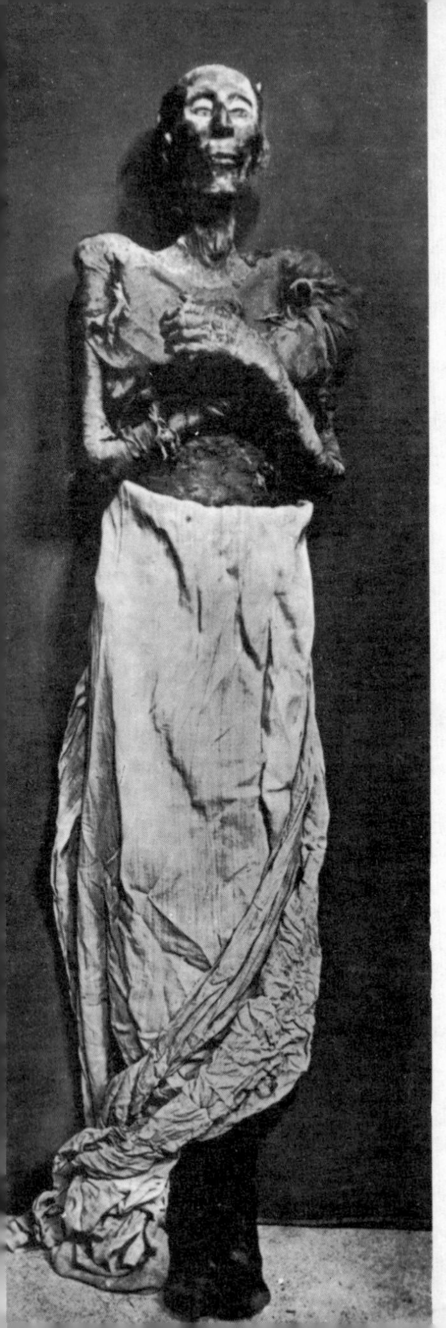

victories neighbouring peoples whom he never touched or dominated (some kings even add the names of people by whom they were vanquished!).

Taken as a whole, there is nothing remarkable about this chronology. Yet it has a certain interest, because there is no century in the history of Egypt which is better known than that of the Rameses. And this does not only refer to its political events but also, and especially, to its social and economic structure. It has been possible to describe everyday life in Egypt by taking the age of Rameses II as typical. And our knowledge of Egyptian society sheds a vivid light on the everyday life of Moses and the Hebrews which the Bible describes. If the chronology of the fifteenth century offers a rich background, that of the thirteenth century gives us detail. The former directs our attention towards political and religious events, the latter towards the social situation.

The empire ruled by Rameses has the rigid hierarchy characteristic of an absolute government. Already the Middle Empire had abolished the feudal

The mummy of Rameses II

system and centralized all power in the person of the Pharaoh. The New Empire preserves this absolutism and develops it into an almost totalitarian state, in the service of which vast masses of human beings are forced into strictly separate classes, each with its definite function within the whole. If we enquire into the state of the lowest classes, we find that at the time there was in Egypt an actual gradation in misery.

First of all there was what historians call the Egyptian proletariat. Here they are using a very modern term to designate a social group which actually existed under the nineteenth and twentieth dynasty in Egypt, showing the identical characteristics of their nineteenth- or twentieth-century European counterparts. Those who belonged to this class were destitute of everything except their hunger: 'We are putrefying with hunger.' That is the only language possible to describe the utter misery under Pharaohs bearing the name of Rameses. These words recur like a leitmotiv, like an obsession on the lips of the proletariat who have nothing else, or almost nothing else to say. Their whole

A bearer of offerings

existence, all that is left to them of personality is summarized almost brutally in the few words of the papyrus of Turin: 'For the last eighteen days we have been putrefying with hunger. . . . We have come, driven by hunger and thirst. We have no clothes, we have no oil, no fish, no vegetables. . . .' These ravenous men are no idlers on the hands of a society which is not responsible for them, since they contribute nothing to it. These are the artisans, the workmen, the peasants, the men and women who enable the people of Egypt to feed, to dress, to build houses and palaces, to trade and to develop their industries. The very fact that these Egyptians who have full rights in their state should have been exploited to such an extent justifies us in calling them proletarians. This exploitation is aggravated by two factors rendering their condition as proletarians even more like that analysed by Karl Marx. All ages and all forms of government have witnessed abnormally low wages for the working classes; they have seen them deprived of even this vital minimum by dishonest practices; the exchequer has only too often seized the cloth woven by the women and the corn grown by the peasant. The famous bas-relief which shows an Egyptian peasant lying full length on the ground, being beaten by the agents of the treasury, evokes the Middle Ages or the last years of Louis XIV rather than the nineteenth century. However, many lesser-known papyri reveal to the amazed reader a psychology of the Egyptian proletarian which is only found in the most modern of states. On discovering this vegetating and empty life one is instinctively reminded of Zola or Gorki: 'Inside the houses the weaver is more unhappy than a woman. He is doubled up so that his knees reach his stomach. He cannot get at the fresh air. It is only by bribing the guards at the door that he can get out. . . . The dyer spends his time cutting rags, he hates clothes. . . . The shoemaker is very unhappy; he is constantly begging; his health is like that of a dead fish; he chews leather in order to keep body and soul together. . . . As for the mason, his two arms are worn out with labour, his clothes are untidy; he nibbles at himself, his fingers are his bread; he only washes once a day. He bootlicks in order to please. He is a pawn passing from one field to the next, each six cubits by ten; he is a pawn passing from one month to the other on the beams of a scaffolding. When he has his bread he goes home and beats his children.' This life, which lacks all individualization and is biologically closed in upon itself, is the first factor which allows us to identify the Egyptian plebeians with the proletariat. The second is the fact that these plebeians are again biologically completely separated from the upper classes. The following text was written by one of the scribes: it is by no means out of sympathy with their plight that he describes the miserable state of the plebeians, but in order to warn his pupils from choosing such a calling. He writes, 'The plebeians stink', and his words are as brutal as those of the proletarian who says, 'I am putrefying with hunger.' Between the privileged scribe and the worker there seems to be no other connection than this stench, this mixture of putrid exhalation, sweat and filth. The man of high birth only recognizes the lowly by the characteristic stench which makes him hold his nose. It is an infernal dialectic which couples the cry of hunger to an instinctive recoil from a stinking breath, and which makes disgust the only possible reaction to misery.

But even now the last depths of Egyptian misery have not been sounded. There are too many indications that the proletariat in Egypt, however unfortunate their actual condition, still remained within the borders separating man from the beast. This refuse of society was still somehow within the pale of justice, not in the shape of well-defined juridical or moral rights, but because there were important psychological factors which at times allowed the plebeians an objective human value. The patriarchal system and revolt are the two main means by which the Egyptian proletariat, without losing its identity, yet proved to be above the lowest rung of the social ladder. The patriarchal system: not all householders reacted in the manner of the scribe. Like Bakenkhonsu, one of the great priests of Amon, some boasted that they had been good fathers to their subordinates, that they had lent a hand to the unfortunate, and helped the needy in their struggle for a living. In the cult of Osiris the deceased had to be able to declare among other things: 'I have never forced anyone to work every day beyond his strength', in order to merit absolution from the god and be found worthy of survival. No worker has testified to the truth of these confessions or the efficacy of these recommendations. But at least they show that the permanent misery of the proletariat roused sporadic pricks of conscience in their exploiters; which prove that, at least theoretically, the proletariat was not divested of all human value. On the other hand frequent revolts among the proletarians of Egypt as well as the patriarchal system show there was still a loophole out of this rigid system. First came the public expression of their grievances—a long papyrus contains those of the peasants, who try in vain to obtain justice in the labyrinth of the royal administration. Then came strikes, provoked by unjust breaking of labour contracts and, above all, by inadequate food supplies. Finally we have regular revolts, pillaging of depots or temples, termed acts of brigandage and sacrilege by official Egyptian historians. The empire is shaken by this muffled underground movement, which reveals the proletariat as a living and active social force. Revolt does not risk remaining in the realm of pious dreams, as the possibilities of the patriarchal system do: it is the inalienable weapon of the exploited. As the powers of Egypt did not know or even wish to utterly destroy the high dignity of man in the proletarian, they left it to him. He remained a man who, though dying of

hunger, could still feed on hope; a man of whom the wisdom of Egypt used to say, 'He still has a heart'.

Yet there were people in Egypt to whom even this last refuge of humanity was denied. And here we find a misery which surpasses even that of the proletariat. If the proletariat remains within certain limits these are overstepped the moment we approach the serfs. Of the slaves, the Egyptian says: 'They have no hearts', and here, as everywhere else in the orient, the heart signifies the personality itself. This discovery, which is as positive as a law of physics, authorizes him to treat the serf like an inanimate object.

These slaves constitute one densely packed mass of humanity. In Egypt the proletariat is numerous. However, in their drawings there are spaces round the peasants and workmen who, in spite of their numbers, seem to retain a minimum of individuality. On the other hand the scenes depicting slavery and forced labour are brutal in their massiveness. Human beings are so closely packed and piled upon each other that they appear as a single whole yoked as such to its work, without any individuality at all.

These human masses are the victims of the totalitarian empire of the Rameses and their passionate and fanatical cult of

power. The State and its prestige demand the systematic construction of colossal depots, fortresses, palaces, temples, cities and tombs. The slaves provide the gratuitous and inexhaustible pool of labour for this immense task.

A name appears here which brings us back to the Hebrews. In the texts from the age of Rameses, groups of foreign slaves, who are compelled to do forced labour of the most exacting nature, are referred to as Apiru. This word is as disturbing as the term Habiru, for it is impossible to know whether it only designates the Hebrews or is used in a wider sense, denoting a group to which the Hebrews belong. It is probable that the Egyptians included the Syrians, Mittanians, Lybians and Arabs; that is, a whole swarm of mixed races, in the word Apiru. But it is likely that the Hebrews shared the fate of the Apiru. As pariahs marked by the hatred of everything Asiatic, they too, like the Apiru, are bound to the pitiless drudgery demanded by the economic expansion of Egypt. If we really wish to appreciate the achievement of Moses, we must realize that in a totalitarian society the Hebrews occupied the lowest place. Together with the Apiru they had reached the uttermost depths of misery.

The reader will appreciate that we refrain from choosing between the two chronologies not from mere prudence, but in the interests of the study of Moses. In both reckonings we must recognize the dominating factors, which are, after all, not contradictory. It is important to know that a relationship between Hebrews and Habiru, as suggested by the left-hand column, is possible. We gain through it our knowledge of the political and religious aspects of the Exodus. But we must not leave the suggestion of the right-hand column, that the Hebrews were the Apiru, out of sight. The Exodus was also (should I say above all?) a social upheaval. The text of the Pentateuch is solidly framed and singularly enlightened by the two chronologies. We have established a complete background which can be referred to, without losing touch with the necessarily complex nature of a Biblical hero.

Rameses III striking down prisoners (Thebes)

The Calling of Moses

On beginning the spiritual biography of Moses we should, if we followed the classical pattern of such studies, treat the man and his achievement separately. However we shall do nothing of the sort. Besides what could be added on the *human* level to the Biblical text which has just been summarized? Novelists, poets, psychologists, all of them more skilful than we, have attempted to interpret the 'illustrious life' of Moses. In spite of them, we are bound to return to the story of the Bible, the tone of which is after all far more accurate than even the best of paraphrases. If a reader wished to know *what kind* of man Moses was, it would be sufficient to recommend an attentive reading of the Bible.

Yet it is a question not exactly of finding out what kind of a man Moses was but rather that he *was a man*. The whole understanding of his personality actually depends on the comprehension of his *humanity* in which the individual and his work are inextricably interwoven.

One could only separate his life and his work by identifying the latter with some form of 'invention of monotheism' which is quite alien to the Bible. From the authentic viewpoint of Biblical theology Moses 'invented' nothing. The God of his fathers reveals himself to this Levite in complete accordance with a long tradition. Any reader who would at this juncture expect learned enquiries into the 'monotheism' of Moses (into his Egyptian, Midianite, Quenite origins; the henotheistic, monolatrous, monarchical elements in his teaching; into his primitive tribalism, and moral universalism) has no legitimate reason to feel disappointed. We consider all these questions as outside our subject. And if anyone wants to devote a study to monotheistic spirituality, he ought to centre it methodically round Abraham, who was the teacher not only of Moses but of Jesus and Muhammad as well. Moses is not the founder of a 'religion', and one would look in vain in the Pentateuch for the elaboration of a doctrine or a theology. He has been called by God, and the Pentateuch gives us an echo and a trace of this call.

His work lies in his vocation. It is a drama that has been lived and is not, consequently, the development of a doctrine. It is our task to show the stages in this drama. But first of all we must trace it to its source in the humanity of him who was called.

The humanity? There is no more convincing illustration of this than the death of Moses. It may be valuable to compare Moses with some of the great 'founders of religion'; with Jesus, with Buddha, or Muhammad, but such comparisons are cut short when it comes to the death of the 'founder'. For Jesus death was the consummation of his whole vocation and the crucial sign of his incarnation and his divinity; for Buddha it was the consummation of his mystical life and the attainment of the shores of liberation. For Muhammad it was a fulfilment which was followed by his transfiguration by legend. For Moses death meant the accomplishment of his life on earth. Although it had been foretold, it came as a surprise. Although it was serene and quite undramatic, it did spell suffering for him, because he was frustrated in the desire of his heart:

> And I besought the Lord at that time, saying, O Lord God, thou hast begun to shew thy servant thy greatness, and thy strong hand: for what god is there in heaven or in earth, that can do according to thy works, and according to thy mighty acts? Let me go over, I pray thee, and see the good land that is beyond Jordan. . . . But the Lord said unto me, Let it suffice thee; speak no more unto me of this matter. Get thee up into the top of Pisgah, and lift thine eyes westward and northward, and southward, and eastward, and behold with thine eyes: for thou shalt not go over this Jordan . . . but I must die in this land, I must not go over Jordan. . . . So Moses the servant of the Lord died there [on the summit of Nebo] in the land of Moab, according to the word of the Lord. And he buried him in the valley in the land of Moab over against Beth-Peor: but no man knoweth of his sepulchre unto this day. And Moses was an hundred and twenty years old when he died: his eye was not dim, nor his natural force abated (Deut. 3: 23–7; 4: 22; 24: 5–7).

In other cases death means fulfilment, achievement, a passing to higher things. Here it means a sudden break: it is a disturbing, a mysterious, a victorious death. It forces Moses to remain alone. Even in the kiss Moses is face to face with the Inexorable. 'Moses did not reach Canaan because his life was too short, but because it was a human life' (Kafka, *Diary*, 19 October 1921). By his death Moses was riveted to the earth. It is his death which from the wrong side, as it were, sheds a light on the meaning of his life and makes of it a symbol of human life on earth.

We must not let ourselves be blinded by the hagiographer's art. The halo of the wonder-worker which has surrounded Moses since the Plagues of Egypt, and, even more, his forty days' fast on the summit of Sinai; his family life, which seems so undeveloped and unimportant when compared with the full-blooded and colourful life of the Patriarchs in Canaan; finally the transfiguration of his face, which makes him the only man in the Bible to be distinguished by a halo: all this does in no wise detract from his humanity for it is safeguarded by certain main virtues. One of the most important of these, when it is mentioned, the Bible makes a sign of the very *humanity* of Moses: his *humility*. 'Now the man Moses was very meek, above all the men which were upon the face of the earth' (Numbers 12: 3). In this verse the translation cannot render the intentional nuances of the Hebrew text. The Hebrew terms used for man and earth have a physical connotation: they evoke Adam, that simple creature, kneaded out of dust and clay. Now Moses was the meekest of all these creatures. There is indeed nothing more simple than the figure of this prophet, who needs no dreams or trances, trembling or ecstasies to receive the revelation of God, but who speaks with Him as a man would to his neighbour. Moses dispenses with that exaltation which is characteristic of prophecy and shows an external analogy to folly. He dispenses with it deliberately. He refuses to 'play' the prophet, the exceptional being, the man who is the depository of secrets to which he alone has the key. His face is radiant: he ignores the fact. When men draw back from him and he learns that his face shines he suffers, and covers it with a veil. He does not attempt to exploit the strange gifts which God has bestowed upon him in such abundance, by surrounding his person with a mystical light. He has nothing of the initiator or mystagogue; there is nothing ambiguous, equivocal or enigmatic in his words and actions. He is not the man who would give the impression that he was cut out for a superhuman destiny. His gift of prophecy appears so natural to him that he is astonished that all men do not prophesy as well (Numbers 11: 29). His meekness has effaced all traces of jealousy and spiritual egoism so well that he has not even any disciples to whom he might reveal his secrets in an intimacy which is reserved for the chosen few. Joshua is his page, his lieutenant in war, but not his disciple. When Moses appoints him as his successor it is a political event and assumes nothing of the air of mysticism which surrounds the scene between Elijah and Elisha. Moses 'initiated' Joshua as little as he did his own children. The teaching of this Master was addressed to all. His metaphysical revelations, however extraordinary and startling, are of a public nature, not less than his judgements in court and political decisions. This injection of supernatural energy into the daily life of a normal society is not the least significant indication of the *humanity* of Moses.

But there are others. The invincible and fundamental human nature of Moses breaks forth in sudden flashes. We can recognize them immediately by their violence: I am referring to his sudden outbreaks of *anger*.

This wrath of Moses! Like all other signs of a passionate nature, it scares well-meaning people, who expect the 'men of God' to be all honey and sweetness. But a little familiarity with the real nature of the Bible is enough to make one understand that these violent outbursts of wrath are the surest sign of a quest for the absolute. It is a painful quest, because it is not granted to man to reach the goal. That is why Moses has these frequent outbreaks; and that is why he remains so perfectly human, because he has kept his thirst for the absolute.

For Moses the absolute bears various names. During the lengthy first period of his life, when Moses does not yet know God and is simply one man among others, his absolute is justice. In a brilliant sketch Ahad Haam has shown that at that period Moses was haunted and spurred on by the idea of justice. The Bible has nothing else to tell of him but a series of scenes, when

Moses rises and intervenes whenever he meets any injustice. He intervenes when the Hebrews quarrel, and tries to force them to separate. He protects the young Midianite girls and saves them from the brutality of the shepherds. He is never at peace; injustice attracts him like a magnet. And since there is no end to injustice, the wrath of Moses is only fully calmed when he deliberately leaves the company of men to withdraw into the solitude of the desert of Midian.

The absolute is still his ideal. Moses reacted with bitterness and anger to the shattering discrepancy between reality and the ideal. In the bitter irony of his 'Why?' (Exod. 5: 22) human sorrow reaches its height. Moses has just been charged by God with a simple, precise and definite task: he is to save the Hebrew people from the clutches of Pharaoh. And now, after his meeting with Pharaoh these fangs enter even more deeply into the flesh of the Hebrews, making them suffer even more. This is the paradoxical revenge of reality: the ideal which has been mocked appears in grotesque distortion. Instead of faces radiating hope and joy Moses meets among his brothers the expression of pain and hatred. Why, *why did You send me*?

But the moment when Moses realizes the gap between reality and the ideal most fully, is doubtless the one when he breaks the Tables of the Law at the foot of Sinai. This is a turning point in Biblical history. On descending the mountain Moses knows already that the people are worshipping the golden calf. God has revealed it to him, and his imagination is at liberty to play on the scandalous proportions of this betrayal. Moses also knows that however great the sin God has pardoned it in advance. He has already forgiven it. Thus Moses descends the mountain, the Tables under his arm, with a double assurance on the ideal plane. He need not be afraid of any surprise as far as reality is concerned, for this would not outstrip his imagination. Besides it must in any case give way before the Divine pardon. Yet the confrontation with reality is so brutal that it annihilates all considerations of the ideal. Even the most fertile imagination could not have conceived of such a horror. Even the most sublime of graces vanishes before such a defiance. The scandal is so immense, reality so provoking, the calf and the Law are so mutually exclusive, that something must be broken, shattered, destroyed. The thirst for the absolute shows itself here in its most intense form: as the refusal to compromise. The integrity of man demands all or nothing. There is no grander or austerer expression of it than the gesture of Moses when he breaks the Law.

When all is said and done, Moses identifies the absolute with God. As he thirsted after justice and the ideal, and his thirst was unquenched, so it is with God. In no other metaphysical experience are the limitations of our humanity better safeguarded than in that of Moses. It is true that his prophetical vocation was extraordinarily eminent. It brought him close to God, with whom he spoke intimately like a friend. The verses in the Bible describing their intercourse suggest a relationship which far surpassed the run of the ordinary:

> And there hath not arisen a prophet since in Israel like unto Moses, whom the Lord knew face to face (Deut. 34: 10). And the Lord spake unto Moses face to face, as a man speaketh unto his friend (Exod. 33: 11). If there be a prophet among you, I the Lord will make myself known unto him in a vision, I will speak with him in a dream. My servant Moses is not so; he is faithful in all mine house: with him will I speak mouth to mouth, even manifestly and not in dark speeches; and the form of the Lord shall he behold (Num. 12: 6–8).

Yet however near this man may be to God, he remains essentially different to God. There is no identification between Moses and the Divine Absolute, neither by way of incarnation, nor fusion nor assumption. This is a postulate of the dialogue character of Biblical prophecy. Metaphysical bilocation is respected in its integrity. The dialogue between God and Moses was clearer in its lucidity than that of the other prophets. Nevertheless the fact remains that it took place between two radically different beings.

In another section we have endeavoured to analyse the structure of the moving drama enacted between God and the prophet, so we may be excused for not dwelling on it for too long now.

Moses on the summit of Sinai (Haggadah of Amsterdam)

Let us simply mention that all the categories which are essential to prophetic service can be found in Moses. Is not the expression 'the servant of God' itself characteristic of Moses throughout the Pentateuch? Moses is a servant by virtue of his initial vocation. The famous scene of the burning bush is one of the most typical in the Bible. When elsewhere a man endeavours to escape God, he puts forward only one or two valid excuses. Jeremiah pleads his youth; Jonah his fear of the Divine repentance. Or like Ezekiel he can only put a frightened silence against God. But Moses pleads his independence with untiring obstinacy. His arguments follow each other in swift succession. They are of unequal weight, but the same tenacity: 'Who am I? Who are you? Who will hearken to my voice? I am not eloquent', down to this last prayer: 'Send . . . by the hand of him whom thou wilt send.' It has no longer any rational motivation, but reveals the anguish of Moses, tracked down like game in the last refuge of its liberty. In this last refuge God takes hold of him and bends him to His will. Henceforth Moses will bear the weight of his vocation. Furthermore Moses is a servant by the suffering this vocation entails, by the dangers it involves, by the doubts it raises in his mind. He doubts his own ability; he doubts the clarity of the divine commands; he doubts the sense and value of his life. Sometimes these doubts take him to the very brink of despair. He wants to abdicate, even to die. But always the next day brings him nothing but new unrest and a new struggle.

Finally Moses is a servant by virtue of his knowledge. Knowledge, in the Biblical sense of the word, does not mean a discovery of the hidden mystery of the Divine Essence; it means the intuitive and penetrating experience of a Presence. An all-too-unknown scene from the life of Moses reveals this problem of the knowledge of God in the Bible.

> Moses said . . . if I have found grace in thy sight, shew me now thy ways, that I may know thee. . . . Shew me, I pray thee, thy glory. And he said, I will make all my goodness pass before thee, and will proclaim the name of the Lord before thee. . . . And he said, Thou canst not see my face: for man shall not see me and live. . . . There is a place by me, and thou shalt stand upon the rock: and it shall come to pass, while my glory passeth by, that I will put thee in a cleft of the rock, and will cover thee with my hand until I have passed by: and I will take away mine hand, and thou shalt see my back; but my face shall not be seen. . . . Be ready by the morning, and come up in the morning unto Mount Sinai, and present thyself there to me on the top of the mount. . . . And Moses rose up early in the morning, and went up unto Mount Sinai. . . . And the Lord descended in the cloud, and stood with him there, and proclaimed the name of the Lord. And the Lord passed before him, and proclaimed, The Lord, the Lord, a God full of compassion and gracious, slow to anger, and plenteous in mercy and truth; keeping mercy for thousands, forgiving iniquity and transgression and sin: and that will by no means clear the guilty; visiting the iniquity of the fathers upon the children, and upon the children's children, upon the third and upon the fourth generation. And Moses made haste, and bowed his head toward the earth, and worshipped (Exod. 33: 13–34: 8).

Then that 'side' of God which approaches man is not His Essence. The knowledge of the Divine Face was denied to Moses, because he was a man and mortal. But the back of God is revealed to man in the glowing appeal of a Love which demands a response down to the third, fourth and thousandth generation. The knowledge of the prophets consists in having been surprised here and now by this Divine challenge. It is their vocation to have been challenged to the conquest of the Absolute in this exhilarating combat with a Living Partner. Man rises from this combat, of which the most typical example is the struggle of Jacob with the Angel (Gen. 32: 25–33), with a heightened consciousness of his humility and vulnerability: Jacob was lamed. However this lameness, this wound, does not mark the end of his existence. In wounding him in what he is, the Absolute restores him to what he may become: Jacob is henceforth Israel. In proportion to his realization that he is contingent, a man's power increases. By the very humility to which he is bound Moses discovers, as did the other prophets, the riches of his vocation.

The struggle between Jacob and the Absolute lasted only one night: the struggle of Moses lasted one hundred and twenty years. Throughout his life on earth Moses searches and throws light upon the presence of God near men. He reveals three fundamental aspects of this presence, which are inscribed in the Pentateuch not in the shape of a theological treatise but as the expression of personal experience. We must find them in the soaring flight, which took him from his beginnings as a child, rescued from the Nile, to the summits of Sinai and Nebo. They range round the important periods of the life of Moses, with the Exodus, the Revelation and the March through the Desert as focal points. In trying to sound the rhythm of this flight we shall find that the values which are revealed by him are too vast to be encompassed by a religion. Great ideas become distinct, which do not only affect faith alone, but the whole of life. I mean the discovery of the Neighbour, of the Law, of the Covenant.

EXODUS:

THE DISCOVERY OF THE NEIGHBOUR

Now there arose a new king over Egypt, which knew not Joseph. And he said unto his people, Behold, the people of the children of Israel are more and mightier than we: come, let us deal wisely with them; lest they multiply, and it come to pass, that, when there falleth out any war, they also join themselves unto our enemies, and fight against us, and get them up out of the land. Therefore they did set over them taskmasters to afflict them with their burdens. And they built for Pharoah store cities, Pithom and Raamses. But the more they afflicted them, the more they multiplied and the more they spread abroad. And they were grieved because of the children of Israel. And the Egyptians made the children of Israel to serve with rigour: and they made their lives bitter with hard service, in mortar and in brick, and in all manner of service in the field, all their service, wherein they made them serve with rigour.

And the king of Egypt spake to the Hebrew midwives, of which the name of the one was Shiphrah, and the name of the other Puah: and he said, When ye do the office of a midwife to the Hebrew women, and see them upon the birthstool; if it be a son, then ye shall kill him; but if it be a daughter, then she shall live. But the midwives feared God and did not as the king of Egypt commanded them, but saved the men children alive. . . . And Pharaoh charged all his people, saying, Every son that is born ye shall cast into the river, and every daughter ye shall save alive (Exod. 1: 8–22). And Pharaoh said, Behold, the people of the land are now many, and ye make them rest from their burdens. And the same day Pharaoh commanded the taskmasters of the people, and their officers, saying, Ye shall no more give the people straw to make brick, as heretofore: let them go and gather straw for themselves. And the tale of the bricks, which they did make heretofore, ye shall lay upon them; ye shall not diminish aught thereof: for they be idle; therefore they cry, saying, Let us go and sacrifice to our God. Let heavier work be laid upon the men, that they may labour therein; and let them not regard lying words. And the taskmasters of the people went out, and their officers, and they spake to the people, saying, Thus saith Pharaoh, I will not give you straw. Go yourselves, get you straw where ye can find it: for nought of your work shall be diminished. So the people were scattered abroad throughout all the land of Egypt to gather stubble for straw. And the taskmasters were urgent, saying, Fulfil your works, your daily tasks, as when there was straw. And the officers of the children of Israel, which Pharaoh's taskmasters had set over them, were beaten, and demanded, Wherefore have ye not fulfilled your task both yesterday and to-day, in making brick as heretofore? Then the officers of the children of Israel came and cried unto Pharaoh, saying, Wherefore dealest thou thus with thy servants? There is no straw given unto thy servants, and they say to us, Make brick: and, behold, thy servants are beaten; but the fault is in thine own people. But he said, Ye are idle, ye are idle: therefore ye say, Let us go and sacrifice to the Lord. Go therefore now, and work; for there shall no straw be given you, yet shall ye deliver the tale of bricks. And the officers of the children of Israel did see that they were in evil case, when it was said, Ye shall not minish aught from your bricks, your daily tasks (Exod. 5: 5–19).

In Egypt bricks are the raw materials *par excellence*. In the great building periods the demand for bricks is practically unlimited. Private houses, civil and military buildings both require more bricks than stone; the walls surrounding the kitchen gardens in the Delta are made of bricks; the mighty wall of the fortified cities are made of brick. In this department work continues without stopping. The workmen are permanently busy. In order to make bricks you have to mix the mud of the Nile with sand and chopped straw, then moisten the mixture, trample on it, stir it with a pick, put it into a mould and, having removed the mould, let the bricks dry. This is hard, tiring work, as it exacts the repetition of the same movements. It is one of the few examples of the conveyor belt in antiquity. The fact that this hard labour should have been demanded from a group of slaves is still consonant with the rational principle prevailing in a totalitarian state, of making full use of its man-power. As the buildings rise from the ground, they prove that this hard labour is economically necessary and corresponds to a demand.

But what necessity constrains Pharaoh to refuse the Hebrews their supply of straw, without which they cannot make bricks; to oblige them to look for this straw themselves and to demand at the same time that they should deliver the same quantity of bricks at the end of the day as before? Here work is not even exacted for reasons of utility. The time taken up in this search for raw materials cannot be made up and the building must inevitably be slowed down. In consequence of such a measure the economic situation of the country must deteriorate. What does it matter? What is at stake is clearly beyond the comprehension of the city. Economic considerations do not come into play: this labour, exacted for its own sake, is meant to crush the men engaged in it, or rather to humiliate them. With this decree of Pharaoh we leave the clear realm of economic laws and pass on to the dark and obscure ones of concentration camps.

Did the Egyptians persecute the Hebrews primarily because they wanted to humiliate them, or did they really intend to exterminate them completely? This question is badly expressed, no doubt: the mysticism of hatred rarely establishes a list of its objectives. What is characteristic of it is the obstinacy with which it forces itself to realize them all. Pharaoh's decrees,

Thebes (Tomb of Rekh-mi-Rhe)

which remind one of Malthus—strangling of the male children by the midwives, drowning of all the male children—are plainly features of a policy for the crime of race-extermination. The victim is struck, body and soul, and the very totality of the attack indicates that it was perpetrated in the world of the concentration camp. Here barbed wire encloses those who are at the same time the guinea pigs of degradation and condemned to death.

Nagging, cruelty, reprisals—of course these are never completely explained by their political context. We can add to them an element of exhibitionism, which brings the most brutal instincts of man into play. Work at the conveyor belt, forced labour, fatigue parties are easily controlled; the taskmasters perform a purely mechanical function. Besides, clocking-in machines have taken the place of the taskmasters of yore. But this humiliating labour is a spectacle. The victims are the actors and the taskmasters are the happy spectators. In this field there is no development. Here brute man remains throughout the centuries on the unchangeable level of his instincts. In Egypt as well as in Auschwitz the whip was the sign of active supervision, of the participation of the spectator in the game played by the

Auschwitz (*'The Book without a Name'*)

Auschwitz ('*The Book without a Name*')

victim. The fact that half of these taskmasters are Egyptians, the other half taken from among the Hebrew victims themselves, is another sign that we are dealing with the world of the concentration camp. You cannot humiliate a victim more surely than by picking him out from among the others and giving him an illusory power, a power only acquired by a consenting to a minimum of treachery, only preserved by a maximum of base acts and only exercised in constant fear of its loss. And eventually it is lost through a sudden caprice which cannot be foreseen or foiled. Sadism does not only release the instincts of the torturer. In itself it contributes effectively to the humiliation of man by man.

Sadism and genocide are twin aspects of the world of the concentration camp. They can be found elsewhere in history. What brings Egypt and Auschwitz so close together is not only the fact that violence was done to the same *people*, but that it was in both places a carefully planned violence. The concentration camps of the Third Reich were governed by 'practitioners of violence', as H. Marcuse so aptly called them. Pharaoh's attack on the Hebrews shows the same familiarity with evil,

Thebes (Tomb of Nakht)

the same calculated and methodical efficiency (Exod. 1: 10). Perhaps there was a foundation of panic and instinctive self-defence, which were seeking some kind of outlet, in the first reaction of the Egyptians. But as time went on, the Egyptian persecution of the Hebrews became methodical, following a distinct plan, the stages of which are traced in the account given in the Book of Exodus and which fit so well into the general framework of the totalitarian New Empire.

Let us recall the physical side of the misery of the Hebrews: exhausting forced labour, the murder of their children at birth, searches, efforts of concealment and abductions, cruelly punished when the attempt failed; officially sanctioned sadism, pitting a man against his brother in a psychosis of mutual distrust and hatred; growing families in a small province, where this population, increasing in spite of adversity, is closely packed: all this in a country where the exploitation of the proletariat, of the foreigners and the slaves was strictly planned. The misery of the Hebrews can only be described as a circle in the inferno of a concentration camp.

Moses broke this circle. He made a breach in this monolith of human misery.

The significance of his deed does not only lie in its immediate consequences. The rift in the Egyptian Empire caused by the Exodus may have been great; the good fortune that befell the fugitive and liberated Hebrew people may have been extraordinary, yet something more essential had happened: a curse, which weighed on wretched humanity and had assumed tangible form in Egypt, was broken. All the values of misery were overthrown, and the men, in whom they were incarnate, were swept along in this movement. The slave, the stranger, the exile, the proletarian had on that day their humanity restored to them. The historical importance of this event lies in the fact that the movement rested on the lowest social stratum, and the lever dislodged the most diverse forms of misery. It was not Israel alone that survived as a result of the Exodus but, with Israel, humanity as a whole. The breach thus formed will in future times provide an outlet for all misery. Throughout history it constitutes an eternal challenge to violence.

Moses threw down his challenge with full knowledge and autonomy. It is true, in the decisive events connected with the Exodus, that he is only the helper of God: but, in killing the Egyptian slavedriver (Exod. 2: 11–12), he prepares the breach which Divine intervention will later enlarge. This murder of the Egyptian bears witness to the way in which Moses meets violence. Here he anticipates in one single act of wrath all that the Exodus will later realize prudently and patiently. Witnessing an injustice and a degradation of man, he feels the blow dealt at the other as though it were directed against himself. Breaking through the selfishness of his own ego, he discovers his neighbour. It is this discovery which, in the last resort, brings about the Exodus. The estrangement between men has disappeared. Before all men were *strangers*, bearing not even the slightest resemblance to oneself. Now all men are *neighbours* and friends.

Everybody. Even God.

'As a man speaketh unto his friend' (Exod. 33: 11), such is henceforth the dialogue between Moses and God. Such is henceforth the dialogue between men and God at Sinai: 'I am the Lord thy God, which brought thee out of the land of Egypt, out of the house of bondage' (Exod. 20: 2). The Exodus from Egypt and that alone authorizes God to say *I* and to call man *Thou*. This metaphysical intimacy has its origin and its justification in the work of God on earth. The way leading from God to men passes through the filth and misery of the crucible of bondage. The Biblical dialogue between God and man follows an essential pattern. Its preliminary is not the justification of man before God, but the justification of God before man.

The whole Biblical account of the Exodus tends towards the reduction of events to a historical level. Evidently the drama enacted in Egypt has mythical proportions. These plagues, these miracles, these frogs, this vermin, this hail and darkness, surely give the impression that they are *signs* of a mythological symbolism opposing, in one of those vast theomachies so familiar to the religions of the Ancient Orient, another mythological symbolism, represented by the sphynxes, bulls, ibises, cats, vultures of Osiris and Horus, incarnate in the person of Pharaoh. And yet, in proportion as it is seen to be historical fact, the myth disappears as in a breath of fresh air. The whole set-up of the narration shows that we have here one of the most typical instances of Biblical *demythologizing*. At the outset, by virtue of their mythical powers, Pharaoh and the magicians hold their own against God. But soon the finger of God appears. The magicians disappear (8:15), and finally the man-god breaks down too. What is left of gigantic Pharaoh with his hardened heart is only a poor mortal, shuddering to learn, at the deathbed of his firstborn son, that he is only a man (12: 30). This is the moment when the way to escape is finally open, and the mass of slaves can blaze a trail towards liberty. Here the Paschal drama is rid of all mythical elements and enacted on the historical level of human life. By virtue of the Passover, 'Upon their gods also the Lord executed judgements' (Numbers 33: 4). All powers of divinization are lost. The hand of God no longer extends towards myths but towards men, in order to strike, to liberate, and to make them equal. God enters the arena of history. The metaphysical encounter blends with the brutally physical breaking of the chains of slavery in the Passover. 'I have broken the bars of your yoke, and made you go upright' (Lev. 26: 13).

COVTE ISRAEL.
I
E SVIS LE SEIGNĒ
TON DIEV. QVI T'AY
TIRE DE LA TERRE
D'EGIPTE DE LA MAIS
DE SERVITVDE. TV
N'AVRAS POINT D'AV
TRES DIEVX DEVANT
MA FACE. TV NE TE
FERAS POINT D'IDOLE
NI D'IMAGE TAILLEE
NY AVCVNE FIGVRE
POVR LES ADORER.
II
TV NE PRANDRAS PO
LE NOM DV SEIGNĒ
TON DIEV EN VAIN. CĀ
LE SEIGNEVR TON DI
EV NE TIENDRA PO
INT POVR INNOCENT
CELVY QVI AVRA PRIS
LE NOM DV SEIGNĒ
SON DIEV EN VAIN.
III
SOVVIENS-TOY DE
SANCTIFIER LE IOV
DV SABATH.

IV
HONORE TON PERE ET
TA MERE, AFIN QVE T
SOIS HVREVX, ET Q
TV VIVES LOG. TE
SVR LA TERRE.
V
TV NE TVERAS
VI
TV NE COMMETT
POINT FONICATIO
VII
TV NE DEROBER
POINT.
VIII
TV NE DIRAS POIN
FAVX. TESMOIGN
CONTRE TON PROC
AIN
IX
TV NE DESIRERAS
POINT LA FEMME D
TON PROCHAIN.
X
TV NE DESIRERAS
POINT SA MAISON
SON SERVITEVR
SA SERVANTE NY
BOEVF NY SON
NY AVTRE
LVY APP

REVELATION:
THE LAW IS GIVEN

The significance of what has happened is not completely revealed in Egypt. The Exodus is only the beginning of the road, but the road has a definite direction: it leads to Sinai. Here God speaks to a whole people. The scene is memorable, and indeed unique in Biblical history; its framework is a theophany which contains all the elements essential to such a numinous experience.

> And it came to pass on the third day, when it was morning, that there were thunders and lightnings, and a thick cloud upon the mount, and the voice of a trumpet exceeding loud; and all the people that were in the camp trembled. And Moses brought forth the people out of the camp to meet God; and they stood at the nether part of the mount. And mount Sinai was altogether on smoke, because the Lord descended upon it in fire: and the smoke thereof ascended as the smoke of a furnace, and the whole mount quaked greatly (Exod. 19: 16–18).

The Decalogue is pronounced, ten majestic commandments. But they are only the foundations of a far more comprehensive spiritual structure. This is gradually composed in the intimacy of a dialogue between God and Moses after the theophany of Mount Sinai. The dialogue continues until that last day when, before his death, Moses can entrust the whole *Law*, faithfully transcribed in the Book and already provided with a lengthy commentary by himself, to the keeping of his people. This Law is the focus of the Sinaitic Revelation. God Who speaks to man as a complete equal since the Exodus does not say *Thou*, but *Thou shalt*. The imperative has appeared: it is inscribed in the stone tablets of the Decalogue, which Moses, bearing them confidently, places in the Ark of the Covenant. It is also inscribed in the *Torah*, which Moses hands to Israel in the serene conviction of having thereby given to men the key to every human vocation.

This imperative can only be explained by a circular dimension, of which it is the centre but not the whole, and certainly

Moses and the Decalogue by Philippe de Champagne

not the complete radiation. But before explaining this in more detail, it is worth while to study the imperative in itself.

Moses, who is the first apologist of the imperative of the Law, underlines its ideal significance and universal grandeur.

> For this is your wisdom and your understanding in the sight of the peoples, which shall hear all these statutes, and say, Surely this great nation is a wise and understanding people. . . . And what great nation is there, that hath statutes and judgements so righteous as all this law, which I set before you this day? (Deut. 4: 6–8)

This day? From a distance of more than three thousand years and without any apologetic intentions, our knowledge of the world as it is enables us to subscribe to this praise of his Law, expressed by Moses.

The imperative of the Law is meant to bring a break with all that went before.

> After the doings of the land of Egypt, wherein ye dwelt, shall ye not do: and after the doings of the land of Canaan, whither I bring you, shall ye not do: neither shall ye walk in their statutes. My judgements shall ye do, and my statutes shall ye keep, to walk therein (Lev. 18: 3–4).

The way of the Law is intended to be an entirely new trail blazed through virgin forest without any contact with previously established orders. Israel's closest neighbours in the desert are Egypt and Canaan. But together with these all the contemporary civilizations of the Middle East are equally rejected. The Torah with its imperative claims to establish a new dimension in an already well-organized world, where men have worked out their religious systems as well as their way of life and thought. Here is not the place to substantiate this claim. This has been done frequently enough by scholars of all descriptions, ever since the juridical and religious texts of the Middle East have, in increasing numbers, become available (the codes of Hammurabi, of the Sumerians, and of the Hittites; the tablets of Ras-Shamra). The conclusions reached are so similar that it is not necessary to treat them in detail.

It may, however, be worth while to draw attention to some of the more remarkable innovations and definite breaks with past practices brought about in the fundamental structure of human society by the imperative of the Torah.

First of all there is the charter of human dignity, laid down in the Decalogue, which is indissolubly associated with the Exodus. It is as though the law, in a desire to prevent the petrification of the Exodus and its relegation into past history, demanded from man when faced with his neighbour, that he put himself back in the situation when the breach was first made: to rediscover the experience of passing from degradation to dignity in all its freshness.

> For the Lord your God, he is God of gods, and Lord of lords, the great God, the mighty, and the terrible, which regardeth not persons, nor taketh reward. He doth execute the judgement of the fatherless and the widow, and loveth the stranger, in giving him food and raiment. Love ye therefore the stranger: for ye were strangers in the land of Egypt (Deut. 10: 17–20). And a stranger shalt thou not wrong, neither shalt thou oppress him: for ye were strangers in the land of Egypt. Ye shall not afflict any widow, or fatherless child. . . . If thou lend money to any of my people with thee that is poor, thou shalt not be to him as a creditor; neither shall ye lay upon him usury. If thou at all take thy neighbour's garment to pledge, thou shalt restore it unto him by that the sun goeth down: for that is his only covering, it is his garment for his skin: wherein shall he sleep? (Exod. 22: 21–7). When thou dost lend thy neighbour any manner of loan, thou shalt not go into his house to fetch his pledge. Thou shalt stand without, and the man to whom thou dost lend shall bring forth the pledge without unto thee. And if he be a poor man, thou shalt not sleep with his pledge: thou shalt surely restore to him the pledge when the sun goeth down, that he may sleep in his garment. . . . Thou shalt not oppress an hired servant that is poor and needy, whether he be of thy brethren, or of thy strangers that are in thy land within thy gates: in his day thou shalt give him his hire, neither shall the sun go down upon it; for he is poor, and setteth his heart upon it. . . . Thou shalt not wrest the judgement of the stranger, nor of the fatherless; nor take the widow's raiment to pledge: but

Lev. 19: 33–4: *And if a stranger sojourn with thee in your land, ye shall not do him wrong. The stranger that sojourneth with you shall be unto you as the home-born among you, and thou shalt love him as thyself; for ye were strangers in the land of Egypt.*

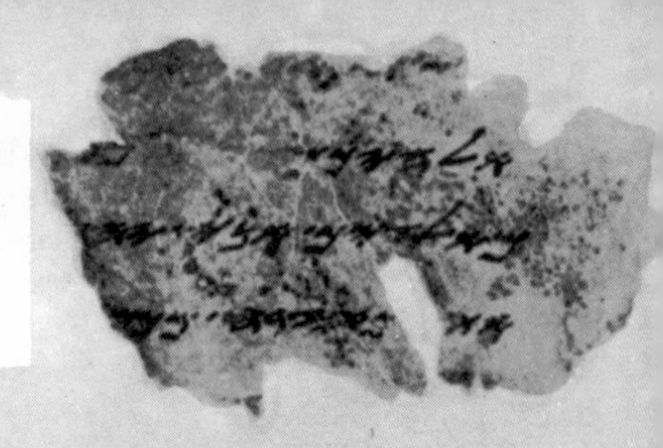

Lev. 20: 22: *Ye shall therefor keep all my statutes, and all m judgements, and do them: that th land, whither I bring you to dwe therein, vomit you not out.*

Lev. 21: 24: *So Moses spake unto Aaron, and to his sons, and unto all the children of Israel.*

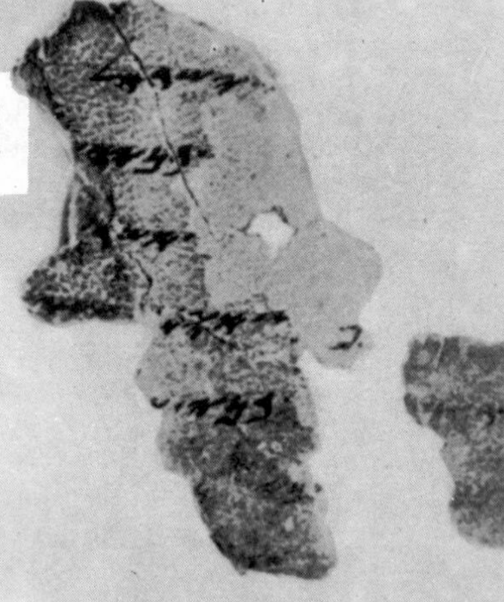

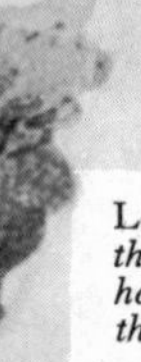

Lev. 22: 4: *What man soever of the seed of Aaron is a leper, or hath an issue: he shall not eat of the holy things, until he be clean.*

thou shalt remember that thou wast a bondman in Egypt, and the Lord thy God redeemed thee thence: therefore I command thee to do this thing. When thou reapest thine harvest in thy field, and hast forgot a sheaf in the field, thou shalt not go again to fetch it: it shall be for the stranger, for the fatherless, and for the widow. . . . When thou beatest thine olive tree, thou shalt not go over the boughs again: it shall be for the stranger, for the fatherless, and for the widow. When thou gatherest the grapes of thy vineyard, thou shalt not glean it after thee: it shall be for the stranger, for the fatherless, and for the widow. And thou shalt remember that thou wast a bondman in the land of Egypt: therefore I command thee to do this thing (Deut. 24: 10–22).

By connecting our neighbour permanently with the authority of a real historical event, the Law can radically change the status of certain groups of people. It is true that the widow, the fatherless and the poor man are only victims of chance, which may be changed for the better the next day. But what about the slave, the foreigner? Is their condition capable of alteration? Do they not represent at the very heart of the social structure of the ancient world a class of men chained to an inescapable fate? The Law gives the slave and the foreigner a definite status. It strictly limits the rights of masters and host nations both with regard to their extent and their duration. It safeguards the autonomy of the individual. In doing so the Law breaks down one of the most tenacious prejudices of group mentality.

If thou buy an Hebrew servant, six years he shall serve: and in the seventh he shall go out free for nothing. . . . And if a man smite the eye of his servant, or the eye of his maid, and destroy it; he shall let him go free for his eye's sake. And if he smite out his manservant's tooth, or his maidservant's tooth; he shall let him go free for his tooth's sake (Exod. 21: 2, 26–7). If thy brother, an Hebrew man, or an Hebrew woman, be sold unto thee, and serve thee six years; then in the seventh year thou shalt let him go free from thee. And when thou lettest him go free from thee, thou shalt not let him go empty: thou shalt furnish him liberally out of thy flock, and out of thy threshing-floor, and out of thy winepress: as the Lord thy God hath

ragments of Leviticus in Phoenician script, discovered at Qumran
)ead Sea Scrolls: 5th–3rd cent., B.C.)

blessed thee thou shalt give unto him. And thou shalt remember that thou wast a bondman in the land of Egypt, and the Lord thy God redeemed thee: therefore I command thee this thing to-day (Deut. 15: 12–15). Thou shalt not deliver unto his master a servant which is escaped from his master unto thee: he shall dwell with thee, in the midst of thee, in the place which he shall choose within one of thy gates, where it liketh him best: thou shalt not oppress him (Deut. 23:15–16). And if a stranger sojourn with thee in your land, ye shall not do him wrong. The stranger that sojourneth with you shall be unto you as the homeborn among you, and thou shalt love him as thyself; for ye were strangers in the land of Egypt (Lev. 19: 33–4). One law shall be to him that is homeborn, and unto the stranger that sojourneth among you (Exod. 12: 49). Ye shall have one manner of law, as well for the stranger, as for the homeborn (Lev. 24: 22).

In admitting the slave, the foreigner and the poor man to the status of 'persons', the Law had to concern itself also with the regulation of labour. It completely overthrows the ancient idea of a horizontal line, which for ever separates the 'leisured classes' from the 'workers', in favour of an alternation of work and free periods, to which all are subject. No man is for ever chained to his work. The periodic and obligatory time of repose is a testimony to his essential liberty.

Six days thou shalt do thy work and on the seventh day thou shalt rest: that thine ox and thine ass may have rest, and the son of thy handmaid, and the stranger, may be refreshed (Exod. 23: 12). Observe the sabbath day, to keep it holy, as the Lord thy God commanded thee. Six days shalt thou labour, and do all thy work: but the seventh day is a sabbath unto the Lord thy God: in it thou shalt not do any work, thou, nor thy son, nor thy daughter, nor thy manservant, nor thy maidservant, nor thine ox, nor thine ass, nor any of thy cattle, nor thy stranger that is within thy gates; that thy manservant and thy maidservant may rest as well as thou. And thou shalt remember that thou wast a servant in the land of Egypt, and the Lord thy God brought thee out thence by a mighty hand and by a stretched out arm: therefore the Lord thy God commanded thee to keep the sabbath day (Deut. 5: 12–15).

The Law formulates another set of commands, which, though less closely connected with the Exodus itself, are no less fundamental: they are connected with sexual morality. The provisions are all the more revolutionary since sexual aberrations of all kinds (homosexuality, bestiality, prostitution, orgies) were not only tolerated by the ancients but even integrated in their religious rites and liturgical worship. The Law condemns them unconditionally as well as their substitutes: magic and superstition. These commands, in which moral precepts are indissolubly bound to the cult, constitute one of the most 'prophetic' parts of the Law.

'eth, the ninth letter of the Hebrew alphabet. Initial f the word tov, *good; middle letter of the word* heth, *in. The two hands indicate the paths of good and evil Abraham Krol: Homage to Scripture)*

There shall be no harlot of the daughters of Israel, neither shall there be a sodomite of the sons of Israel (Deut. 23: 17). And thou shalt not give any of thy seed to make them pass through the fire to Molech, neither shalt thou profane the name of thy God. . . . Thou shalt not lie with mankind, as with womankind: it is abomination. And thou shalt not lie with any beast to defile thyself therewith: neither shall any woman stand before a beast, to lie down thereto: it is confusion. Defile not ye yourselves in any of these things: for in all these the nations are defiled which I cast out from before you: and the land is defiled: therefore I do visit the iniquity thereof upon it, and the land vomiteth out her inhabitants. Ye therefore shall keep my statutes and my judgements, and shall not do any of these abominations; neither the homeborn, nor the stranger that sojourneth among you (Lev. 18: 21–6). When thou art come into the land which the Lord thy God giveth thee, thou shalt not learn to do after the abominations of those nations. There shall not be found with thee any one that maketh his son or his daughter to pass through the fire, one that useth divination, one that practiseth augury, or an enchanter, or a sorcerer, or a charmer, or a consulter with a familiar spirit, or a wizard, or a necromancer. For whosoever doeth these things is an abomination unto the Lord: and because of these abominations the Lord thy God doth drive them out before thee. Thou shalt be perfect with the Lord thy God (Deut. 18: 9–14).

The 'spirit of the prophets' is likewise to be found in the demand for justice and charity, which is so astonishingly polarized in the Law. We must pursue justice, heeding no obstacles, not the sanctuary of a Temple, not the established power, nor the tears of charity.

That which is altogether just shalt thou follow (Deut. 16: 20). And if a man come presumptuously upon his neighbour, to slay him with guile; thou shalt take him from mine altar, that he may die (Exod. 21: 14). Ye shall not respect persons in judgement; ye shall hear the small and the great alike; ye shall not be afraid of the face of man; for the judgement is God's (Deut. 1: 17). Thou shalt not wrest the judgement of thy poor in his cause (Exod. 23: 6). Thou shalt not follow a multitude to do evil (Exod. 23: 2). Neither shalt thou favour a poor man in his cause (Exod. 23: 3). Ye shall do no unrighteousness in judgement: thou shalt not respect the person of the poor, nor honour the person of the mighty: but in righteousness shalt thou judge thy neighbour (Lev. 19: 15).

But the commandment of love is just as absolute. We must overcome the psychosis of hatred, break down all social prejudices, and shatter the bonds of selfishness.

If thou meet thine enemy's ox or his ass going astray, thou shalt surely bring it back to him again. If thou see the ass of him that hateth thee lying under his burden, and wouldest forbear to help him, thou shalt surely help with him (Exod. 23: 4–5). The stranger that sojourneth with you shall be unto you as the homeborn among you, and thou shalt love him as thyself (Lev. 19: 34). Thou shalt not take vengeance, nor bear any grudge against the children of thy people, but thou shalt love thy neighbour as thyself (Lev. 19: 18).

At no point does the Law show a bolder sweep, however, than in the command of sanctity. None of the well-known sociological definitions of sanctity (formal piety, heroic virtue, asceticism) can cover the famous nineteenth chapter of Leviticus, where the commands affect the most surprising collection of contrasting realities. Body and soul, spirit and will, moral conscience and natural instinct, time and space, the individual and society, morality and the liturgy are mentioned side by side with a disconcerting promiscuity, the principle of which would remain obscure were it not for the key provided by the second verse: 'Ye shall be holy; for I the Lord your God am holy.' Men are thus invited not only to obey: they are invited to imitate. The Torah cannot be reduced to an imperative. It aims at another way, at participation, the first step towards which lies in imitation. This idea of imitation sheds some light on the nineteenth chapter of Leviticus, which shows how human sanctity can be achieved by imitating the sanctity of God. The whole aim and content of the Law is life. In the life of God the One, the sanctity of God is realized. But must man, who was created to the image and likeness of God, remain incomplete, torn by the infinite number of contradictions in his life? The

Law illuminates human life in its entirety, or rather it enfolds life like a gigantic wave, flowing through all its openings, infiltrating through all its channels, and spreading between all its banks. From the most brutal of biological instincts to the most refined spiritual sublimation, all is embraced by the Law and impregnated by it. If the manifold aspects of life are intimated with such realism, it is because the effort to attain sanctity must tend towards their organization and unification.

> And the Lord spake unto Moses, saying, Speak unto all the congregation of the children of Israel, and say unto them, Ye shall be holy: for I the Lord your God am holy. Ye shall fear every man his mother, and his father, and ye shall keep my sabbaths: I am the Lord your God. Turn ye not unto idols, nor make to yourselves molten Gods; I am the Lord your God. . . . And when ye reap the harvest of your land, thou shalt not wholly reap the corners of thy field, neither shalt thou gather the gleaning of thy harvest. And thou shalt not glean thy vineyard, neither shalt thou gather the fallen fruit of thy vineyard; thou shalt leave them for the poor and for the stranger: I am the Lord your God. Ye shall not steal; neither shall ye deal falsely,

nor lie to one another. And ye shall not swear by my name falsely, so that thou profane the name of thy God: I am the Lord. Thou shalt not oppress thy neighbour, nor rob him: the wages of a hired servant shall not abide with thee all night until the morning. Thou shalt not curse the deaf, nor put a stumbling block before the blind, but thou shalt fear thy God: I am the Lord. Ye shall do no unrighteousness in judgement: thou shalt not respect the person of the poor, nor honour the person of the mighty: but in righteousness shalt thou judge thy neighbour. Thou shalt not go up and down as a talebearer among thy people: neither shalt thou stand against the blood of thy neighbour: I am the Lord. Thou shalt not hate thy brother in thine heart: thou shalt surely rebuke thy neighbour, and not bear sin because of him. Thou shalt not take vengeance, nor bear any grudge against the children of thy people, but thou shalt love thy neighbour as thyself: I am the Lord. Ye shall keep my statutes. Thou shalt not let thy cattle gender with a diverse kind: thou shalt not sow thy field with two kinds of seed: neither shall there come upon thee a garment of two kinds of stuff mingled together. . . . Ye shall not eat anything with the blood: neither shall ye use enchantments, nor practise augury. Ye shall not round the corners of your heads, neither shalt thou mar the corners of thy beard. Ye shall not make any cuttings in your flesh for the dead, nor print any marks upon you: I am the Lord. Profane not thy daughter, to make her a harlot; lest the land fall to whoredom, and the land become full of wickedness. Ye shall keep my sabbaths, and reverence my sanctuary: I am the Lord. Turn ye not unto them that have familiar spirits, nor unto the wizards; seek them not out, to be defiled by them: I am the Lord your God. Thou shalt rise before the hoary head, and honour the face of the old man, and thou shalt fear thy God: I am the Lord. And if a stranger sojourn with thee in your land, ye shall not do him wrong. The stranger that sojourneth with you shall be unto you as the homeborn among you, and thou shalt love him as thyself; for ye were strangers in the land of Egypt: I am the Lord your God. Ye shall do no unrighteousness in judgement, in meteyard, in weight, or in measure. Just balances, just weights, a just ephah, and a just hin, shall ye have: I am the Lord your God, which brought you out of the land of Egypt. And ye shall observe all my statutes, and all my judgements, and do them: I am the Lord (Lev. 19: 1–37).

All the same, as we have remarked, the imitation of God is only a step towards the real purpose of the Law: participation. The very word Law is not wide enough to contain the full meaning of the Hebrew term *Torah*. It was only after the translation of Torah as *nomos* in the Greek of the Septuagint that the word Torah came to mean Law. The Hebrew word *Torah* does not signify order but orientation. It is not a Law, it is the way, the road along which a common enterprise is possible.

As a matter of fact, the commands of the Torah are rarely expressed in the imperative mood, but almost always in what Hebrew grammar calls the Imperfect (*im*perfect: what has not yet been achieved). The Imperfect has the character of an invitation rather than that of a command, and implies the equality of the two actors, suggesting an atmosphere of prayer rather than of obedience.

Prayer: this is not saying too much. There is one theme of especial significance in the Torah of Moses, which will prove this beyond doubt. It is the theme of the love of God.

> Thou shalt love the Lord thy God with all thine heart, and with all thy soul, and with all thy might (Deut. 6: 5). And now, Israel, what doth the Lord thy God require of thee, but to fear the Lord thy God, to walk in all his ways, and to love him, and to serve the Lord thy God with all thy heart and with all thy soul, to keep the commandments of the Lord, and his statutes, which I command thee this day for thy good? (Deut. 10: 12–13)

It is true, other great leaders of the ancient world had already guessed, if not clearly expressed, the fact that God loves men, that he is their father, their protector, their patron. But that men should be invited to love God, was a discovery which changed the religious pattern of the world completely. It seems as though in his Torah God revealed his demand for love because he needed love. The whole Covenant is marked by this quest for love, and since Sinai its exultant and at the same time fearful character is very marked. From Adam to Noah, from Noah to the patriarchs, from the patriarchs to Sinai, God has been ceaselessly seeking his people. Now, on Sinai, he has definitely found them. The nostalgia of God is relieved. God has a plan which he wishes to realize together with men: he calls upon them to co-operate with him. The Torah is simply the statement of the efforts necessary to ensure the success on earth of a common adventure between God and men. It is the Charter of the Kingdom of Heaven on earth. 'Ye shall be unto me a kingdom of priests, and an holy nation, for all the earth is mine' (Exod. 19: 6).

A kingdom of priests! That is the keynote of the Torah. Until that day men had been wrong about the meaning of the world. They had thought that it belonged to them: now the world belongs to God. Men had lived in the illusion that they were the owners of their estates: now these estates belong to God. They had at least thought that a human kingdom had a sacred authority: now God is the sole authority, He alone is king. These errors were discovered in Egypt. The illusion was dispelled. Human might crumbled before the word of God. Now the last consequences of the Exodus must be accepted and the reconstruction of the world according to the new data, announced in the Torah, faced with a set purpose. 'The earth is mine. You are my farmers and tenants. I am King!'

Yet the Torah does not demand that the world should annihilate itself before God, but rather that it should be transformed, in order to receive Him. It need not give up its vocation on the physical level: rather it must open itself to the metaphysical. The route the Torah marks out does not lead from a city of men to a city of God. Within the limitations of human life it leads from the isolation of God and men to their sharing a common city.

Long chapters of the Torah are devoted to elaborating this programme. To the superficial reader they may sound Utopian, but if in fact there have been individuals who have in their lives been able to show that the 'saintly way of life' described in the nineteenth chapter of Leviticus is possible, why should a whole community not be capable of following the collective 'saintly way of life' propounded by the Torah? However that may be, these chapters are characterized by a keen sense of realities. 'Society' is not condemned here in the manner of Rousseau or the ascetics. Its institutions are reorganized, improved and corrected. The Torah criticizes men, not concepts, and it prevents men from doing harm by making it imperative for them to do good, or, to use the very words of the Torah, 'to bring redemption'. We might add, and still remain faithful to the language of the Torah, that it enjoins the 'circumcision of the heart' (Deut. 10: 16; Lev. 26: 41); the avaricious heart of the peasant; the covetous heart of the master; the cruel heart of the hunter; the heart of the creditor; and the heart of stone of the neighbour. But a change of heart does not suffice. The Torah also enjoins the 'circumcision of institutions': the cult is improved by the centralization of all sacrifices in one place; the priesthood by the appointment of the Levites; kingship by messianism.

Finally the Torah announces the 'circumcision of time'. If time were allowed to advance autonomously, the increase of power in the hands of one group and the decay of the others would certainly be as irreversible and irremediable as time itself. The establishment of the sabbatical and jubilee cycles allows for a new beginning as well as for compensations: the so-called *redemptions*. In Hebrew a single term is used: *geulah*, which, in the 25th chapter of Leviticus, includes the ideas of redemption, liberation and restitution.

> And the Lord spake unto Moses in mount Sinai, saying, Speak unto the children of Israel, and say unto them, When ye come into the land which I give you, then shall the land keep a sabbath unto the Lord. Six years thou shalt sow thy field, and six years thou shalt prune thy vineyard, and gather in the fruits thereof; but in the seventh year shall be a sabbath of solemn rest for the land, a sabbath unto the Lord: thou shalt neither sow thy field, nor prune thy vineyard. That which groweth of itself of thy harvest thou shalt not reap, and the grapes of thy undressed vine thou shalt not gather: it shall be a year of solemn rest for the land. And the sabbath of the land shall be for food for you; for thee, and for thy servant and for thy maid, and for thy hired servant and for thy stranger that sojourn with thee; and for thy cattle, and for the beasts that are in thy land, shall all the increase thereof be for food.
>
> And thou shalt number seven sabbaths of years unto thee,

seven times seven years; and there shall be unto thee the days of seven sabbaths of years, even forty and nine years. Then shalt thou send abroad the loud trumpet on the tenth day of the seventh month; in the day of atonement shall ye send abroad the trumpet throughout all your land. And ye shall hallow the fiftieth year, and proclaim liberty throughout the land unto all the inhabitants thereof: it shall be a jubile unto you; and ye shall return every man unto his possession, and ye shall return every man unto his family. A jubile shall that fiftieth year be unto you: ye shall not sow, neither reap that which groweth of

Moses carrying the Law (*Abraham Krol*)

itself in it, nor gather the grapes in it of the undressed vines. For it is a jubile; it shall be holy unto you: ye shall eat the increase thereof out of the field. In this year of jubile ye shall return every man unto his possession. And if thou sell aught unto thy neighbour, or buy of thy neighbour's hand, ye shall not wrong one another: according to the number of years after the jubile thou shalt buy of thy neighbour, and according unto the number of years of the crops he shall sell unto thee. According to the multitude of the years thou shalt increase the price thereof, and according unto the fewness of the years thou shalt diminish the price of it; for the number of the crops doth he sell unto thee. As ye shall not wrong one another; but thou shalt fear thy God: for I am the Lord your God. Wherefore ye shall do my statutes, and keep my judgements and do them; and ye shall dwell in the land in safety. . . . And the land shall not be sold in perpetuity; for the land is mine: for ye are strangers and sojourners with me. And in all the land of your possession ye shall grant a redemption for the land.

If thy brother be waxen poor, and sell some of his possession, then shall his kinsman that is next unto him come, and shall redeem that which his brother hath sold. And if a man have no one to redeem it, and he be waxen rich and find sufficient to redeem it; then let him count the years of the sale thereof, and restore the overplus unto the man to whom he sold it; and he shall return unto his possession. But if he be not able to get it back for himself, then that which he hath sold shall remain in the hand that hath bought it until the year of jubile: and in the jubile it shall go out, and he shall return unto his possession. . . .

And if thy brother be waxen poor, and his hand fail with thee; then thou shalt uphold him: as a stranger and a sojourner shall he live with thee. Take thou no usury of him or increase; but fear thy God: that thy brother may live with thee. Thou shalt not give him thy money upon usury, nor give him thy victuals for increase. I am the Lord your God, which brought you forth out of the land of Egypt, to give you the land of Canaan, to be your God (Lev. 25).

At the end of every seven years thou shalt make a release. And this is the manner of the release: every creditor shall release that which he hath lent unto his neighbour; he shall not exact it of his neighbour and his brother; because the Lord's release hath been proclaimed. . . . Beware that there be not a base thought in thine heart, saying, The seventh year, the year of release, is at hand; and thine eye be evil against thy poor brother, and thou give him nought; and he cry unto the Lord against thee, and it be a sin unto thee. Thou shalt surely give him, and thine heart shall not be grieved when thou givest unto him (Deut. 15: 1–2; 9–10).

Moses knows full well that this project requires much patience and a strong will. He fears the temptations arising from the earth, from power, from pride. In spite of this, as though to prove that the realization of these ideas is indeed possible, the camp of Israel at the foot of Sinai in the desert is organized like a miniature city of God. In it God dwells among his allies in the tent of meeting. He is their only leader. The arrangements in the camp are described in full detail. Have we not here a prefiguration of the city of God? And are not the people serving their apprenticeship for it?

Here an unforeseen obstacle arises. Even long before the Promised Land with all its attractions is reached, the city of God is shaken and threatens to disappear altogether during the highly dramatic crisis in the desert.

THE DESERT: THE COVENANT BETWEEN GOD AND HIS PEOPLE

'Moses and the desert': the words are said and misunderstood as quickly as 'Moses and Egypt'. In order to grasp the significance of the subject and extract its real meaning, the following simple statement is useful; in the life of Moses there is not only *one* desert, there are two. Geographically speaking it is the same peninsula with the mountain range of Sinai as its backbone, and the two arms of the Red Sea as its borders. However in this arid desert, with its infrequent oases and its countryside parched by the sun, Moses lived through two completely different sets of experiences. The first occurred between his murder of the Egyptian and his return to Egypt; the second, much later, when he was leading Israel to the land of Canaan. The two periods are all but equal in length—each lasted about forty years. The radical difference between the two experiences is emphasized by the similarity in time and space. All the conditions seem realized for the same man to lead the same kind of life in the same place, after the lapse of a few months. Yet this similarity is completely overshadowed by the incontestable peculiarities of the two ways of life, each of which, without disowning the influence of the desert, gives it a different significance.

The day after he murdered the Egyptian Moses finds solitary refuge in the desert. In an oasis of Midian he meets a wealthy and wise man, whose daughter he marries. She bears him two children. But all this is quickly cut short. On his return to Egypt on the back of his donkey Moses is again alone. For when Moses fled from Egypt, it was not only because he was a hunted man. The desert does not open itself up to him as a shelter or refuge, as to an outlaw. The desert welcomes a man who has been betrayed, betrayed by Egypt, whose injustice has roused his conscience; betrayed by his brethren, whose abject cowardice drives him to despair and whose secret accusations threaten him. In fleeing from Egypt Moses has broken with civilization. He is endeavouring to escape the machine which makes men into cogs and which at the time functioned with such immovable precision in Egypt. The desert calls him: it is a place of solitude, of silence, of forgetfulness; it is a sacred spot, a natural storehouse, whose fruits, though scarce, satisfy your hunger; whose springs, though rare, quench your thirst. As Moses leads his flocks farther into the desert, his startled conscience finds peace. Soon he is surrounded by an atmosphere of renunciation, of asceticism, of poverty, and of a contented solitude.

Jean Steinmann has shown that such a situation is propitious for all opening up unto the Divine Spirit (*Saint John the Baptist and the Desert Tradition*[1]). In the desert the hermit prepares the harvest of the spirit by embracing holy poverty; by seeking solitude he prepares the Divine encounter. In the desert Moses is in readiness for his vocation. The moment the bush begins to burn, everything becomes clear: the desert has completed its task. A man has found his vocation; a pastoral monologue has been changed into a mystical dialogue. No doubt Moses expresses his surprise, his lack of preparation, his fears, when he is speaking with God. What does that matter? The desert has transformed this man, who made himself a void and a silence. It has filled him to overflowing with spiritual riches, with words and with prayer. Into his very being, betrayed by the world of men, the desert places the world of the Spirit. Here the influence of the desert ceases. God sends Moses back into the world of men, far from the desert. Within its limits of time and space the desert has brought about a mystical adventure. This was its meaning during the long years when Moses wandered over it alone: slowly, secretly, and in his very depths it guided him towards the call, the encounter.

But after the Exodus, during the long years when Moses is once more crossing the same desert, it changes its significance. It now gives shelter to an impressive multitude, to a people of whom Moses is the leader. And this people is to be organized according to principles which cover its political, social, religious and economic life. He intends to educate this nomad people and make it into a veritable city, with magistrates, priests, artisans, woodcutters, and water carriers—with all its tribes

[1] Longmans, 1958. *Men of Wisdom.*

The mystical desert of Sinai

surrounding the Ark of the Covenant and the portable Temple. But the city of Israel is not built without severe setbacks; the new society is only born after painful gestation. The people do not cease to query its component parts, its foundations, and even the principles of its existence. Above all, the question of the leader is put with untiring regularity. The people revolt against him, when he is too unassuming or too authoritarian. They replace him when, apart from them, he delays too long over his prayers. The desire for all kinds of political systems: autocracy, oligarchy, democracy, anarchy, manifests itself in a disorderly fashion. Then the very meaning of the expedition is questioned. Now the people stay idle, now they are over-hasty. Now they retrace their steps, now they obstinately rush in the direction of defeat. Between these two extremes there are the usual experiences of a people on the march: wars, revolts, vast hecatombs and exciting resurgences. Moses is caught in the turmoil of such a life. In this desert there is no more solitude for him. Instead, he is faced with a harassing social mission, an uninterrupted activity, the perpetual claims of an over-excited multitude. This is quite a different desert with a different purpose to the one which Jean Steinmann attributes to Moses, as the precursor of John the Baptist. Half a century of experiments in collective living, with its needs, its psychoses, its evolutions, its changes, its failures and its successes—all these, the marks of pulsating human existence, are written on the sands of the

The desert and its multitudes

desert. This is not the desert familiar to the spiritual life. It is the desert of a real and concrete objective history.

These are contradictory, yet not mutually exclusive, aspects of the same desert. And it is in this very juxtaposition that the genuine 'desert' of Moses appears. For this desert is actually the paradoxical locality where a unique adventure takes place: the Covenant; a Covenant which receives its unalienably double character from the association between God and man. It is at the same time spiritual and physical, mystical and historical.

The mysticism of the desert is not only reserved for Moses in his solitude. The whole motley crowd in all its social and psychological diversity shares an extraordinary mystical experience. In the original plan the desert was meant to be the place of a mystical encounter, not of a long sojourn. God had said to Moses: 'Ye shall serve me here', in the desert. And Moses had repeated it to Pharaoh: 'A three days' journey in the desert, in order to serve God there.' God and Moses hastened to meet again, to hear each other again, to let the whole people share in their dialogue, face to face. The 'service in the desert' is indeed realized. It is, on an enlarged scale, necessitated by the multitude who shared in it, a mystical encounter, resembling the one of the burning bush. The setting is the same—the desert of Sinai. But instead of the bush, the whole mountain is aflame. Instead of a single individual, it is a whole multitude who hear the Voice. Originally the centre of gravity of the whole adventure of the desert was that supreme moment when God and men met. All the rest was accessory to it. The desert was to be crossed rapidly. The plan envisaged an eleven-days' journey, just time enough to advance without delay. The goal was clear: the cultivated land of Canaan. The civilized country of Egypt was left in order to find another as quickly as possible. The desert between the two might have been avoided, and the Biblical text suggests that the route might have been along the coast, avoiding the desert. Yet it was necessary to penetrate into the desert for a few days so that the encounter between God and men could be effected at Sinai. It was a solemn moment, shedding its spiritual light upon the whole journey. The people feed on manna which falls from the sky every day. A pillar of cloud or of fire fixes the stages of the journey, and at the same time marks the space in the desert within which the people are called to live for a few days. God dwells in the midst of his people: the Ark of the Covenant is the spot where the mystical encounter takes place and the centre of this community of hermits and prophets, whose numbers are counted in thousands.

Hermits? The term is ambiguous. It is important to state that the mystical hermitage of Sinai did not sever the links between Israel and the world, but shed an especial light upon them. In conformity with the call sounded even before the revelation of the Decalogue, the Kingdom of God was building on a universal scale: 'For all the earth is mine' (Exod. 19: 5). And actually one can see the neighbouring peoples, the small world of the Middle East, grouping themselves round the people of Israel like the radii of a circle. They all belong to God, but the meaning of their election only becomes clear by virtue of the overriding election of the City of Israel. The existence of this City in the middle of all the others makes it impossible to conceive of the geography of the Middle East in profane terms. Government becomes theocratic in the whole area which, together with Israel, includes Egypt, Canaan, Amalek, Edom, Moab, Ammon, Midian, Philistia and Phoenicia in one moral unity. The criteria of power and failure are no longer physical

The dead of the desert and their resurrection (*original designs by Adèle Wajsman*, 1956)

force or weakness, but virtue or corruption. The idea of the Divine Justice reappears as formidable and exacting as in the charter of the City of Israel. But this time it is on an international scale. And it becomes clear that this vigilance of God is practised from the centre: the encounter between God and one people enables God to encounter them all.

On the reverse of this mystical experience we have the physical side of the desert. Everything happens as though the Hebrews were reacting to their mystical vocation by taking the opposite direction. The limits of their camp are marked by pillars: they are disputed. The people would like to advance, to retreat, to avoid the way God is tracing, in order to choose a human way, regardless of whether it lead to liberty or slavery. The divine bread is offered to them: a gift, which would have satisfied the hermits abundantly, appears scanty and insulting to the starving multitude that have left Egypt. These men suffer the pangs of hunger and thirst in the very marrow of their bones. They must have bread, meat, vegetables, fresh water—tangible food which is substantial, tasty, consistent and full of flavour. The miraculous foundations of their life are constantly despised and trampled upon; so are the morals. The Hebrews judge neighbouring peoples only by externals. They are feared because they are strong. Notwithstanding, they are defied. As their customs are corrupting, their debauchery is shared. The austere theocracy of their government is reduced to a succession of outbreaks of panic, alternating with self-assertion, a veritable parody. Even the mystical moment of Sinai, the dialogue with God is caricatured. Instead of a metaphysical revelation we have the dance round the golden calf.

The real significance of the Covenant consists in the fact that the physical reverse and the mystical obverse of the desert are not mutually exclusive. They are welded together to form the unique *history* of the desert. God does not let men escape him. He does not withdraw in indignation. He does not exterminate them all of a sudden. The dialogue between heaven and earth is not interrupted; it continues. God has not made a rigid plan. He does not stake everything on the success of the mystical adventure. He takes up the challenge of the people, their defiance. He notes their refusal, even anticipates them at times. He corrects, emends and changes his plan. He gives up the idea of a mystical appeal and is ready to play the game on the historical level. On the dewy manna he throws meat; he sends war to the cowards, and defeat to the proud. Sometimes, it is true, he considers breaking all this resistance of men, and of exterminating the whole people, of beginning a purely mystical and miraculous adventure with Moses alone. But in the end, the *historical* will of God prevails, and he continues to the end with *this* people. He is ready to sacrifice to it almost his entire original plan: a journey of forty years instead of eleven days, time for one generation to die and the next to grow up. This death and this birth are not miraculous. The generation of the Exodus does not die in one day, and those who will conquer Canaan do not appear suddenly the next morning. There might have been a 'miracle': the instantaneous death of a multitude and an immediate resurgence. But here as well God assures the historical continuity and contemporaneousness of old men who grow older, and new men who are growing up. Those who died in the desert do not disappear before the living: they lead them for a time, which may differ in length but is none the less real, to the very threshold of the Promised Land.

Among all those who died in the desert Moses leads the living furthest and for the longest time. We can guess the importance of the part he plays in this desert, where the Covenant is made. God takes men seriously. With all its imperfections, its setbacks, its wounded, and its dead, human history has a meaning. It is only Moses whose seriousness can be compared to that of God, and the meaning of the history of the desert was worked out by him as well as by God.

As he occupies the position of a mediator between God and men, Moses is free to make his choice. Now in critical situations, he opts with God for the maintenance of the covenant. He does so not only because he loves this Hebrew people, to whom he is attached. Certainly there is something of the 'good shepherd' about the psychology of Moses, something of the artist, who is proud of his work, and protects and defends it even when it becomes ugly. However, this maternal instinct is sometimes dulled, and God is obliged to reawaken it:

> Have I conceived all this people? have I brought them forth, that thou shouldest say unto me, Carry them in thy bosom, as a nursing-father carrieth a sucking child? (Num. 11: 12)

He has also an intuition of the pedagogical value of the desert, and the lesson this exemplary event teaches.

> And thou shalt remember all the way which the Lord thy God hath led thee these forty years in the wilderness, that he might humble thee, to prove thee, to know what was in thine heart, whether thou wouldest keep his commandments, or no. And he humbled thee, and suffered thee to hunger, and fed thee with manna, which thou knowest not, neither did thy fathers know; that he might make thee know that man doth not live by bread only, but by every thing that proceedeth out of the mouth of the Lord doth man live. Thy raiment waxed not old upon thee, neither did thy foot swell, these forty years. And thou shalt consider in thine heart, that, as a man chasteneth his son, so the Lord thy God chasteneth thee (Deut. 8: 2–5).

However, beyond this intuitive grasp of the pedagogical significance of the desert, Moses shows an acceptance of the risks involved, which is quite irrational. He realizes the fundamental meaning of the adventure of the desert. The dialogue, once started, cannot be broken off again.

> Thou hast avouched the Lord this day to be thy God . . . and the Lord hath avouched thee this day to be a peculiar people unto himself (Deut. 26: 17–18).

What happened in the desert is not fixed in time as a touching memory of things past, nor has it only a catechetical importance: it is like marriage in the life of a couple. It is serious, definite and prophetical. The road which the people followed through the desert leads farther. The Land of Canaan is not only the goal of *this* desert, it is the goal of all the deserts in a history, the pattern of which was traced there *for all time.*

For all time! This expression, which is the leitmotiv of the Pentateuch and the sign of the permanence of the Law and the Covenant, has in Hebrew a special as well as a temporal connotation. It established the Law and the Covenant in all places and all times. Its most literal explanation is given by Moses himself:

> Neither with you only do I make this covenant and this oath; but with him that standeth here with us this day before the Lord our God, and also with him that is not here with us this day (Deut. 29: 14–15).

In several key chapters of the Pentateuch (Lev. 26; Deut. 28, 29, 30, 32) Moses enlarges upon the *prophetical* significance of the desert, regardless of the limits of time and space. These chapters are too lengthy to be reproduced in full here. Yet if they are not accepted, our understanding of the Pentateuch will always be incomplete.

The universality of the message is now assured. Future dispersions of the people will be 'from the one end of the earth even unto the other end of the earth' (Deut. 28: 64); they will return again 'from all the peoples' (Deut. 30: 3). In the original desert the theopolicy only envisaged the people of the Middle East. Now all the peoples between heaven and earth (Deut. 32: 1, 43), those who were present with Moses and those who were not present, are integrated into this history.

And in the centre of this universal history there is *one* people, the very one who were in the centre of the adventure of the desert: the Jewish people, whose astounding perenniality is announced in these chapters with a realism becoming more and more mysterious down the centuries.

> If ye walk in my statutes, and keep my commandments, and do them . . . then I will walk among you, and will be your God, and ye shall be my people. . . . But if ye will not hearken unto me, and will not do all these commandments; and if ye shall reject my statutes, and if your soul abhor my judgements, so that ye will not do all my commandments, but break my covenant . . . then I will scatter you among the nations, and I will draw out the sword after you: and your land shall be a desolation, and your cities shall be a waste. Then shall the land enjoy her sabbaths. . . . And as for them that are left of you, I will send a faintness into their heart in the lands of their enemies: and the sound of a driven leaf shall chase them; and they shall flee, as one fleeth from the sword; and they shall fall when none pursueth. . . . And ye shall perish among the nations, and the land of your enemies shall eat you up. . . . If then their uncircumcised heart be humbled, and they then accept of the punishment of their iniquity; then will I remember my covenant with Jacob: and also my covenant with Isaac, and also my covenant with Abraham will I remember; and I will remember the land. The land also shall be left of them, and shall enjoy her sabbaths, while she lieth desolate without them; and they shall accept of the punishment of their iniquity; because, even because they rejected my judgements, and their soul abhorred my statutes. And yet for all that, when they be in the land of their enemies, I will not reject them, neither will I abhor them, to destroy them utterly, and to break my convenant with them: for I am the Lord their God: but I will for their sakes remember the covenant of their ancestors, whom I brought forth out of the land of Egypt in the sight of the nations, that I might be their God: I am the Lord (Lev. 26).

Exposed as they are to the eyes of all the nations, the Jewish people know that they are also seen by God. And inversely, by grounding the Covenant on the very foundations of history, Moses has engraved the universal vocation of the Jewish people upon the memory of God.

הוי כל צמא
לכו למים

The Vocation of the Jewish People

And there hath not arisen a prophet since in Israel like unto Moses, whom the Lord knew face to face.

Deuteronomy, conclusion.

At Sinai Moses was initiated in the Torah. He transmitted it to Joshua; Joshua to the Elders. The Elders transmitted it to the prophets; and the prophets transmitted it to the men of the Great Synagogue.

Talmud: MISHNAH ABOT, opening.

Hear, O Israel: the Lord our God, the Lord is One. Thou shalt love the Lord thy God with all thine heart, and with all thy soul, and with all thy might. And these words, which I command thee this day, shall be upon thine heart; and thou shalt teach them diligently unto thy children, and shalt talk of them when thou sittest in thine house, and when thou walkest by the way, and when thou liest down, and when thou risest up. And thou shalt bind them for a sign upon thine hand, and they shall be for frontlets between thine eyes. And thou shalt write them upon the door posts of thine house, and upon thy gates . . . that ye may remember and do all my commandments and be holy unto your God. I am the Lord your God, who brought you out of the land of Egypt, to be your God: I am the Lord your God! . . .

True and firm, established and enduring, right and faithful, beloved and precious, desirable and pleasant, revered and mighty, well-ordered and acceptable, good and beautiful is this thy word unto us for ever! . . . His words also live and endure; they are faithful and desirable for ever to all eternity, as for our fathers so also for us, our children, our generations, and for all the generations of the seed of Israel his servants. . . . In the heights of the universe is thy habitation, and thy judgements and thy righteousness reach to the furthest ends of the earth. . . . From Egypt thou didst redeem us, O Lord our God, and from the house of bondmen thou didst deliver us; . . . Wherefore the beloved praised and extolled God, and offered hymns, songs, praises, and thanksgivings to the King and God, who liveth and endureth; who is high and exalted, great and revered, who bringeth low the haughty, and raiseth up the lowly, leadeth forth the prisoners, delivereth the meek, helpeth the poor, and answereth his people when they cry unto him; even praises to the Most High God, blessed is He, and ever to be blessed. Moses and the children of Israel sang a song unto thee with great joy.

Morning Service of the Synagogue, based on *Deuteronomy* 6: 4–9, and *Exodus* 15.

I believe with perfect faith that the prophecy of Moses, our teacher, was true, and that he was the chief of the prophets, both of those who preceded and of those that followed him. I believe with perfect faith that the whole Law, now in our possession, is the same that was given to Moses, our teacher. I believe with perfect faith that this Law will not be changed, and that there will never be any other law from the Creator, blessed be his name.

Seventh, eighth and ninth principles of the Jewish faith formulated by Moses Maimonides (1135–1204).

My beloved is mine, and I am his, the shepherd among the roses. Israel addresses this invocation from the Song of Songs to Moses, who like the ever-faithful shepherd accompanies his people through the roses and also through the briars.

Zohar, mystical interpretation of *Exodus* 3: 1.

Advance and give your name. 'My name? Although it is not my surname, my name is Jew, a word signifying one who praises, and unceasingly glorifies the Sole Being, the Eternal One.' Your age? 'My age? I am two thousand years older than Jesus Christ.' Your profession? 'I leave the sorry professions prepared for me aside. My traditional profession is the following: I guarantee the holy indefeasibility of the name of the Law, and I am the living guardian of the ancient nobility and the legitimacy attached by Divine right to the name, the proper name of the people.'

JOSEPH SALVADOR (1796–1873),
The Law of Moses.

The last lines of the Pentateuch contain a warning for all time against the bold attempt to separate Moses from his message and Israel from their vocation.

SAMSON RAPHAËL HIRSCH (1808–88),
Commentary on the Pentateuch, conclusion.

In every Jewish generation there is a revival of Moses.

AHAD HAAM (1856–1927), *Moses.*

United, inseparably and eternally united, Moses and the Jewish people pass through history. The texts quoted are not only impressive because of their temporal continuity, but for the diversity of their outlook. The Written Law, the Oral Law, the liturgy, dogmatic theology, mystical sensibility, contemporary thoughts of secular, religious or Zionist colouring all combine to bear an eloquent testimony.

Yet these are only gleanings, gathered while the harvest is still continuing. Let us try to analyse the ideas of which the few texts are only examples. We cannot claim to describe them all in full. But at least we can hint at the most significant ones: those which lead straight to the heart of the work of Moses, in the Passover of Exodus, the Revelation of the Law on Sinai, and the Covenant in the desert. Their expansion throughout the ages throws a light on the human mission, the cosmic fidelity, and the Messianic solitude of the Jewish people.

Seder (Haggadah of Nuremberg)

THE EXODUS:

A HISTORICAL MISSION

Jews and Christians both use the word Pasch to describe their feast. The French use Pâque for the Jewish feast and Pâques for the Christian feast. Linguistically the difference is minimal, for its origins are recent.

In the Middle Ages the two expressions were still undistinguished. And in any case they have a common root. Through the Greek *pascha*, both the French form *Pâques* and *Pâque* are phonetical transpositions of the Hebrew *pesach* which, in the Torah of Moses, signifies the night of the Exodus and the feast commemorating it throughout the ages. The theologian, however, would not admit that this differentiation of terms is only due to change. He would rather recognize in it the workings of a profound reality and the sign of a spiritual constellation. Plural and singular reflect an important historical truth.

As a matter of fact both Christian and Jewish spirituality are fundamentally Paschal in their roots. They are Paschal as well by virtue of the sap which, flowing from the root, nourishes their spiritual organisms and brings forth their flowers and their fruit. Through the presence of the Christian and the Jew this Paschal sap has penetrated the whole of western civilization with its flavour. And one might well show how up to a point the values most appreciated by the West—liberty, redemption, resurrection—are Paschal values. The basic event in Judaeo-Christian spirituality is doubtless the night of the Exodus. But Christianity has superimposed another event and thus created two Paschs, while Judaism has retained the event in its original purity. The decisions of the Nicene Council are symptomatic in this respect. On that occasion the Christian Church set out to define its true nature; and its break with Judaism becomes apparent in the changing of the date of Easter. The name of the feast remains, but the feast itself is no longer attached to the full moon of spring (which witnessed the Exodus of Israel from Egypt) but to the Sunday of the Resurrection of Jesus. And this Sunday assumes the place of the Sabbath in the reckoning of holy days. Thus the whole Biblical economy is modified: another meaning is added to the original meaning of the Passover, including and assimilating it, just as an isolated note becomes part of a complete musical composition. Here lies the fundamental conflict between Christianity and Judaism: the Christian message rings out in the bells of Easter: Judaism upholds the absolute supremacy of the first note of the Passover.

This Passover of Moses, to which Judaism has remained essentially faithful, has not been upheld without effort. In an excellent study ('Quand je suis sorti de l'Égypte, Notes sur la Pâque juive', *Evidences*, March 1956), David Jassine shows that even before the advent of Christianity the Jews had yielded to the temptation to *allegorize* the Mosaic lesson of the Passover. In the teaching of its most distinguished member, Philo of Alexandria, Hellenistic Judaism translated the Exodus into idealistic terms: leaving Egypt signifies overcoming matter, entering the world of the soul, passing mysteriously from the somatic to the pneumatic state. Even before Christianity Judaism was ensnared by another temptation: preserving solely the sacrificial rite of the Passover shorn of its historical context. The Samaritans, who were heathens settled in Palestine by Nebuchadnezzar in the sixth century B.C., adopted the Jewish cult without identifying themselves with Jewish history, without having their Temple destroyed, their Land lost, their people exiled. They celebrate the Passover according to the precepts of Moses. Their fidelity is touching, but false. Only lately they were watched by astonished spectators at Nablus in 1948, when the two hundred Samaritans of the twentieth century were forced to disperse and emigrate. These spectators saw before their very eyes a Passover kept to the letter. But it was an anachronism. It was the Paschal rite bereft of the Paschal history.

The Jewish Passover cannot be encompassed by a Hellenistic allegory or Samaritan ritual. The Paschal spirituality of the Jews does not reject all symbolism, but it refuses to raise it to the level of a language which has no longer anything to do with time. It does not reject all ritual. But it forces it, by its amplitude and its historical roots, to avoid all rigidity and to retain a

Medieval Seder (Haggadah of Serajevo)

permanent tension between the past and the present. Thus, half way between the timelessness of pure ideas and the anachronism of a ritual that is fixed in the past, the Paschal spirituality of the Jews expresses itself in the realism of history as Moses had from the beginnings envisaged.

The central act of the Jewish Passover is the Seder, a ceremony which is celebrated in every house round the family table in the night of the full spring moon: 'And this day shall be unto you for a memorial, and ye shall keep it a feast to the Lord: throughout your generations ye shall keep it a feast' (Exod. 12: 14). From the time of the Second Temple the ordinance was established. Jesus of Galilee and his disciples (Mt. 26, Mk. 14, Lk. 22, Jn. 13:26), Hillel the Pharisee (*Talmud Mishnah Pesachim*), Onias the Essene (Qumran Texts) celebrated the Passover as it has come down in the Jewish community to our day. There are hundreds of documents written throughout the centuries in celebration of the Jewish Passover, the Seder. Some are austere and dogmatical, others picturesque and sentimental.

Modern Seder (Kibbutz in Galilee)

We shall quote one taken from a romantic poet of the nineteenth century:

> When night falls the mistress of the house lights the candles; she spreads the tablecloth on the table and lays three of the flat unleavened loaves in the middle, covering them with a napkin. Then she places on this raised surface six small dishes containing symbolic food: an egg, lettuce, horse-radish, a roasted shank bone and a brown mixture of raisins, cinnamon and nuts. The master of the house sits down at this table with all his relatives and companions and reads to them out of a strange book, called Haggadah, which is a quaint mixture of ancestral legends, wondrous stories from Egypt, odd accounts, controversies, prayers and festive hymns. This solemnity is interrupted in the middle by a large supper, and even during the reading some of the symbolic food is partaken of; at the same time small pieces of unleavened bread are eaten, and four glasses of red wine

Washing of hands (Haggadah of Paris; French origin, beginning of 15th cent.)

drunk. This evening ceremony has a melancholy serenity. It is at the same time cheerful and serious, a fairy story and a mystery. And the traditional chant to which the master of the house intones the Haggadah, the burden of which is at times taken up by the listeners, sounds familiar and awe-inspiring, now lulling you to sleep like a mother, now awaking you so suddenly that even those Jews who have long since given up the faith of their fathers and pursued the pleasures and honours of an alien world are touched to the quick, when the old, familiar notes of the Passover happen to strike their ears (Heinrich Heine, *The Rabbi of Bacharach*).

Is this page taken from Heine, this homage paid to the night of the Exodus, as the Jews commemorate it in perpetuity throughout the ages, only the testimony of a poet? There is certainly some truth in it. No other solemnity evokes a similar degree of emotion. The genius of a people displays itself

Seder dish (painted china from Lunéville, 18th cent.)

הודו ליי כי טוב
כי לעולם חסדו
יאמר נא ישראל
כי לעולם חסדו
יאמרו נא בית אהרן
כי לעולם חסדו
יאמרו נא יראי יי
כי לעולם חסדו

naïvely in poetry, art, and music. Everything happens as though this feast enjoyed the privileges of raising up vocations which might otherwise be choked or thwarted by historical circumstances or doctrinal directives. Here the intense intellectualism of the talmudist becomes gentle and supple. Dialectics, exegesis and ritual unfold on the level of a child. The verses from the Bible, the traditional texts, the sacred gestures are purposely naïve and spontaneous. They assure eternal youth to this millennial solemnity. During the Middle Ages the Jews' taste for the plastic arts was blunted, partly as a result of legal proscriptions. But Jewish artists in the Middle Ages—and today—delight in adorning the Haggadah of the Passover. Certain liturgical books are masterpieces; their illustrations are all the more touching as it is known that they were executed within the walls of the ghetto, under the threat of expulsion or execution. It is a strange way of circumventing all prohibitions, which is undoubtedly linked with the intimate, profoundly human character of the family feast, the Seder. For this invites the Jew to find modes of expression which will complete the spoken word, and which are sometimes better able to create a more vivid communion, a simpler and profounder solidarity between the participants and between the generations.

This is also an escape from anguish, however: an evasion into the land of dreams, beyond our human misery. This reserve of emotion and popular art amidst a habit of abstract thinking has a significance beyond the realm of aesthetics. Heine has already mentioned it. He is not only bound to the Jewish Passover by virtue of its poetry. There is a far deeper sentiment. The Passover contains for him a reproach and a challenge. It poses the question which is fundamental to the Jew and challenges him to answer that very question which God addressed to Abraham: 'Where art thou?' The mysticism of the Passover is essentially tragic rather than romantic. The Jew is always more or less a stranger in life. The reality, the gravity, and the meaning of his alienation are measured by the Passover. No Jew can pass the Haggadah untouched. For its style is not narrative, but interrogative. Its story is not told like a legend,

l theme from the Seder (Haggadah MS. of Albert A. Neher and Nathan
', ascribed to Mahannayim. Lanteuil, Corrèze, 1943–4)

but like a problem. One initial question is asked, and all the others follow from it: 'What is the difference between this night and all other nights?' It is for the Jew to answer if he can, and if he cannot, to feel that the question contains a challenge.

Like an unfinished play the night of the Exodus continues through the centuries, seeking actors to relive it perpetually, and to grasp its essential meaning.

> In every century every man has the duty to look upon himself as though he had himself left Egypt. The Holy One, blessed be he, has not only redeemed our ancestors, but us also together with them. For it is written (Deut. 6: 23): And he brought *us* out from thence, that he might bring *us* in, to give *us* the land which he sware unto our fathers.

This passage from the Haggadah might relegate the Passover ceremony of the Jews to the category of repetitive rites had not the underlying myth so concrete a historical translation in each century that each time it is not the Jew who places himself *ritually* in that night in Egypt, but the night of the Passover that

comes to him in all the fullness of a *present-day* problem. Philo disembodied Pharaoh and Egypt, explaining them as mythological. But history has placed innumerable pharaohs of flesh and bone in the path of Israel. It has scattered Israel to the four corners of the universe, enclosing the Jews within the hideous prison walls of many Egypts, loading them with heavy chains inside barbed wire. This explains the striking effect the Passover theme has on the Jewish conscience. The sudden awakening mentioned by Heine is not due to the burden of a familiar ancestral melody; it is due to the fact that a destiny which the Jew believed to have shaken off, rises up before him, and meets him on each Passover night with a force that is torture in itself. It is not the aesthetic attraction of the night alone which causes so many writers to centre their theme of 'the revival of Jewish consciousness' round the night of the Passover; it is its spiritual significance. With a stroke of genius Christopher Fry projected such a spiritual crisis into his play (*The Firstborn*) on the first Exodus. Shendi, the eldest son of Miriam and nephew of Moses, having suffered with the other Hebrews, is promoted. He is a soldier in the Egyptian army, a kapo in the camps, torturing his brothers even more than the Egyptians themselves. But the night of the Exodus comes. Will he die with the firstborn of Egypt, or will the cry, wrung from his very entrails, 'I am a Jew!' be heard? Christopher Fry only raises this question. Yet the whole of Jewish history has answered this cry, which may have been uttered by a Shendi of flesh and blood in the days of Amenophis or Menephta. This unique moment of time, which once and for all separates the world into torturers and victims, into oppressors and liberated, serves as a point of reference for all generations, so that in each generation every man, every Jew, may rediscover his own essential place, even when he has denied and scorned it all his life. Jewish writers, too, could not but let their heroes, Jews who have strayed into neutrality or indifference, find the significance of their Jewishness in the brilliant light of the night of the Passover. (Jo Sinclair, *Identity*; Sammy Tronemann, *Tohu Vabohu*). In almost all the novels dealing with the Marranos the crypto-Jews take

Wherefore is this night different to all other nights?
(Haggadah of Nuremburg)

off their masks and reveal their identity during a Passover night. Moreover, is not the *Rabbi of Bacharach* a confession of a deep remorse? Was it not immediately after his formal conversion to Lutheranism that Heine wrote it? Only Israel Zangwill ends the play on a tragic note, when the Jew feels a stranger to the world of the torturers as well as the world of the tortured. In *Had-Gadya* he describes the final situation of the Jew who is face to face with the Passover. During a Passover which he takes part in at Venice, a young emancipated Jew of the nineteenth century becomes so conscious of the failure and absurdity of his estrangement and, simultaneously, of his inability to identify himself completely with his brothers, that he commits suicide in the waters of the canal, while the last notes of this Passover Haggadah, which touched him to the quick, are ringing through the half-open windows above.

It is obvious, and the above examples, even though they are taken from literary and romantic works, underline the fact that the centre of the Jewish Passover is not the Jewish people as such. Its annual return does not resemble a patriotic festival like the fourteenth of July, the glory of which deserves enthusiasm and even sacrifice. So little is the Seder a national festival that the Haggadah does not even mention the name of Moses the Liberator. No human exploit is indicated. But what is shown as necessary is that the Jew should become conscious of his Jewishness. Not that the members of a nation should unite to celebrate a national liberation, but that the very ideas of liberation and redemption should be removed from the sphere of abstract thought and be considered from the point of view of an experience, *which differs from all others*, the experience of the Jewish people in Egypt. *In all ages, it is the duty of EACH MAN to think of himself as one who had himself come out of Egypt*. What then is the *human* significance of this liberty, which only those can bear witness to who accept the idea of having won it, like Moses, in Egypt?

The first thing that is expressed in the Jewish Passover is the certainty of freedom. With the Exodus a new age has struck for humanity: redemption from misery. If the Exodus had not taken place, marked as it was by the twofold sign of the overriding will of God and the free and conscious assent of men, the historical destiny of humanity would have followed another course. This course would have been radically different, as the redemption, the *geulah* of the Exodus from Egypt, would not have been its foundation. During the night of the Passover the Jew says: 'Neither my fathers, nor I, nor my children would be free; we would still remain slaves for ever.' Inversely, the door opened by the Exodus cannot be closed again. 'We are free with an eternal freedom.' This is a paradoxical certitude, when it is proclaimed by the Jew, who is miserably immured in the Ghetto, caught in the toils of persecution. However, the Jew cannot escape from this paradox by taking refuge in a dichotomy of freedom. He refuses to believe that only moral liberty is eternal, and that physical liberty might be lost for a time. The Jewish Passover respects the universal and indivisible quality of liberty. The Exodus was a physical, social and political event, a liberating of the body as well as of the soul (as a matter of fact rather of the body than of the soul, which was only fully set free on Sinai). The energy which then poured down upon the world like a torrent is inexhaustible and invincible. No barrier can resist it. All constraint is accidental; all misery is only provisional. The breath of freedom which has blown over the world since the Exodus can dispel them this very day. This is the conviction proclaimed by the Jew when he 'breaks bread and raises the chalice of wine' in the night of the Passover: the bread of misery, and the wine of liberty, one vanquished by the other; proclaimed when in the era of the Temple he tasted of the Paschal lamb; when he tastes the bitter herbs, their bitterness overcome by the Passover today. The optimism of the Jewish people, their philanthropy during centuries of patriarchal government, their social dynamism in revolutionary ages have their source and their impetus in the Passover, which retains the sense given it by Moses. 'Whoever is hungry, let him come and eat. Whoever is in need, let him come and celebrate the Passover': this is the invitation at the beginning of the Jewish Passover night. By its 'social' implications it appears to transcend the purely religious sphere, yet it is based on none other than the Pentateuch of Moses. The very fact that the Jewish 'religion' at its most authentic speaks the language of the 'laity', enables all Jews to 'communicate' in the Passover. I have used the word 'communicate' deliberately, as in Christianity the difference between the believer and the non-believer is most noticeable at the Paschal Communion. On the contrary believers and non-believers meet in a common faith during the Seder of the Jewish Passover. And though the Seder celebrated in a religious setting has its marvels, the Seder of Jewish workmen, who are socialists and unbelievers, is no less characteristic of the essential nature of the Exodus and its influence on the historical destiny of Israel.

If the Jewish Passover is faithful to the Pentateuch of Moses in its social interpretation of the Exodus, it also retains its eschatological elements. The idea of *geulah*, which is used indiscriminately in the Torah to signify liberation and redemption, and which simultaneously covers the redemption of the slaves in Egypt in the past and all redemption from an accidental enslavement in the future, is not sublimated in the Jewish Passover. The redemption of the future is intentionally conceived as on the physical and not on the moral plane; it is of this earth, and not of heaven; it is human and not divine. Edmond Fleg has brought out this eschatology of the Jewish Passover very clearly (cf. p. 167). The Supper, which in the Christian dispensation is essentially divine and brings the universe back to God, is in the Jewish dispensation, a human supper, which allows everyone to recover the meaning of his vocation as a man. Such a vocation necessarily involves a realization of the condition of man as such. The event of the Passover allows all its depths and all its heights to be explored. From the dust of the most abject misery to the most fascinating miracle by which human dignity is restored to all its grandeur, the night of the Seder forces man to face and so fight himself. At the end of the dialogue this 'vocation' becomes quite clear. It summons man to join his brother in the building of Jerusalem and, by that very fact, in the rebuilding of the world.

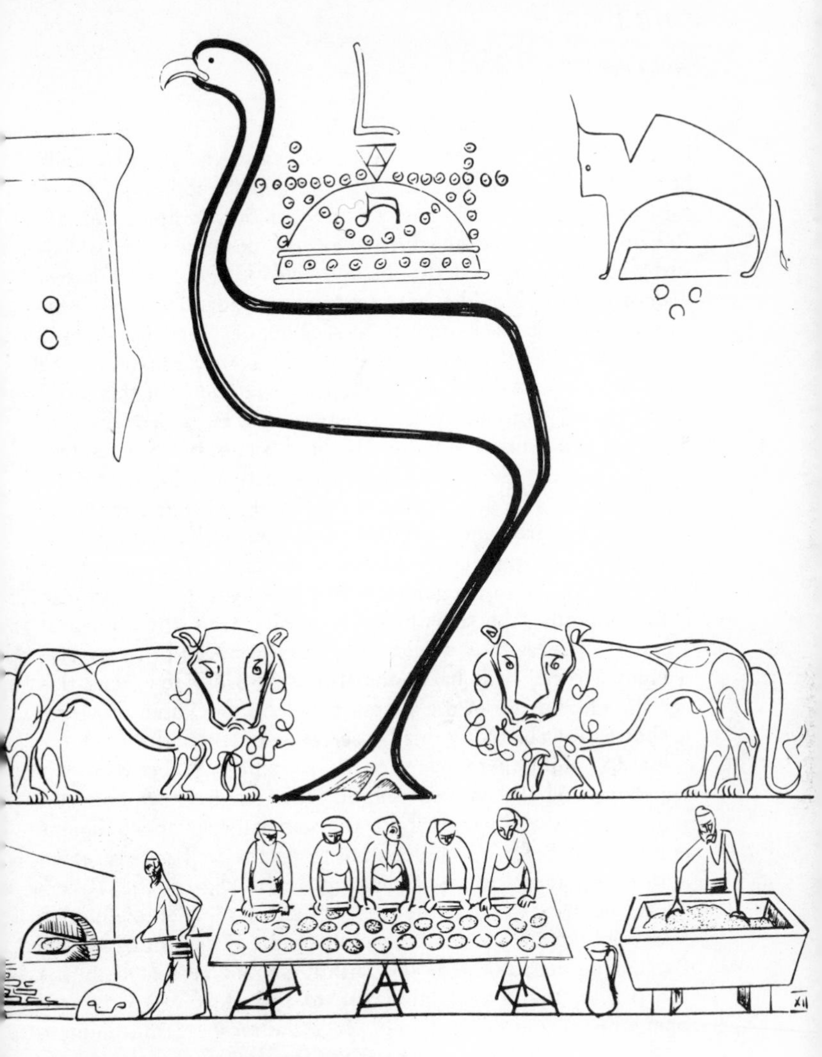

The word liberty begins with the letter L. In Hebrew it is the initial of the word lehem, *bread. Bread of liberty: symbol of the Passover.*
(*Abraham Krol: Homage to Scripture*)

THE LAW:
A COSMIC PLAN

On one of the bas-reliefs of the Arch of Titus in Rome, Roman soldiers, crowned with laurels, carry the sacred vessels of the Temple in Jerusalem in a triumphal procession. There were few ornaments and no statuary in the Temple, and the Romans might have imagined they had destroyed the Jewish rite when they burned the Temple and pillaged its treasures. *Judaea deleta?* No, the holy treasure of Judaea was not destroyed. On his back one of the legionaries carries a simple oblong box doubtless containing a *Sefer Torah*, a scroll of the Law of Moses. At that period thousands of copies of this scroll were extant. A thousand others were soon to be copied. Judaism has lived and continued to live by this forest of books, each tree of which bears the text of the Pentateuch of Moses, and by nothing else. The dimensions of the Torah, with its five thousand eight hundred and forty-five verses, make this scroll heavy, difficult to manipulate, cumbersome to carry. That makes no difference: when in danger Jews first save lives, then—and well before all other possessions—this scroll. It is their greatest treasure. Just as they would rush into the fire in order to save a child, so they will brave the flames in order to rescue this scroll. The fidelity of the Jewish people to the Torah of Moses is shown very clearly by this consecration of an object.

At first sight there seems to be no difference between this hallowing and the halo surrounding the religious symbols and relics of other religions. Like the national flag or a religious emblem, the Sefer Torah demands respect as well as creating an aura of mystery. In the Synagogues it is kept in the Tabernacle, the place which is the centre of devotion. Yet it is hidden from sight by a veil of heavy material. If the ritual of the Synagogue demands that the faithful should be seated during the prayer, the congregation rise to their feet when the veil opens before the Sefer Torah. It is the most solemn moment in the Jewish liturgy: you have the impression of being transported to the foot of Sinai at the moment when the whole assembly of Israel were standing to receive the Word of God.

Hidden from sight by a veil . .

לא יהיה לך
לקדשו
כבד את אבי
ואת אמך
לא תרצח
לא תנאף
לא תגנב
לא תענה
לא תחמוד
מנחם משיב נפשי
לפק

א

This sacred scroll, it is true, is often, as in other religions, surrounded by naïve and even superstitious devotions; but there is a characteristic of it which is peculiar to Judaism. The Sefer Torah is the only book among the sacred books of humanity which demands a traditional transcription. It must be written by hand on parchment. It must conform absolutely to its model, not only as far the text is concerned, but also in the arrangement and composition of the letters. This model, the origin of which goes back to dim antiquity, is said by tradition to have been written by Moses in the desert. Each Jew, at one time, made a copy of the Sefer Torah during his lifetime. It is a peculiar pilgrimage, which does not lead the disciple to a place sanctified by the prophet, but makes him repeat on his own path the gesture by which the message is passed on. This rite has no doubt fallen into disuse, and the majority of Jews entrust its execution to a trained scribe; nevertheless ideally the command still exists, and the minutest breach of the rules for transcription renders the Sefer Torah useless for liturgical purposes. A Sefer Torah which contains even the slightest error, a Sefer Torah in which the ink of even the most commonplace word has faded so as to make it illegible, and (is it really necessary to mention it?) a printed Sefer Torah, are all useless. There is nothing sacred about them but the halo of respect. They are buried, as one buries a dead child. The entire hallowed *life* of the Sefer Torah lies in the scrupulous fidelity of its text to the text of Moses.

For three thousand five hundred years each Sefer Torah seems only to have *lived* in proportion as it has preserved the text of the Law of Moses authentically. Even the most 'liberal' Synagogue has respected this organic character of the Sefer Torah. In the sacred economy of Judaism the Sefer Torah bears witness to the fact that it is not the passage of time nor the breaking up of matter that cause the death of the Law, but infidelity to the text of Moses. When a faithful Sefer Torah dies of old age or by accident, *its letters fly away*, and wait till they are gathered from the air by another scribe who will incarnate them in a new body. The literal text is the soul of the Sefer Torah, and it is eternal like the human soul.

. . *the Sefer Torah is in the Tabernacle*

The text of the Torah is not only the soul of the Sefer Torah, it is also the soul of Judaism. The whole body of the Jewish people and not only the hallowed object in the Synagogue draw their life, their fruitfulness, and their originality only from the presence in their midst of this text. The presence of this *text*: for in face of the Law the only option left to the Jew is to accept its *letter*, and to discover in this letter the permanent and radiating centre of the life of the Law.

This text is so much part and parcel of Jewish life that the Jew encounters it perpetually both in time and in space. The house of the Jew, the intimate framework of his life, bears on the upper part of the right post of its doors the *Mezuzah*, a small parchment on which two passages from the Torah are inscribed (Deut. 6: 4–8, and 11: 13–21). On his body the Jew wears the phylacteries, which are tied to his left arm and his head. They also contain extracts from the Torah (Deut. 6: 4–8 and 11: 13–21; Exod. 13: 1–16). The liturgical day begins with the recitation of the Shema (Deut. 6: 4–8 and 11: 13–21; Num. 15: 37–41) and concludes with it. This Shema marks not only the limits of the Jewish day, but of the entire life of the Jew. It is the first word to be lisped by the child; it is the last on the lips of the dying. In the Synagogue the complete text of the Torah is read on Mondays, Thursdays, on the Sabbath and on feast days, in an annual cycle. Other ritual occasions are linked to this public reading: birth, circumcision, adolescence, marriage, bereavement are as many 'summonses to the Torah', where in principle those who have been summoned read the 'section for the week', or, if they are not expert enough to read it, listen to the reading especially destined for them.

The text of the Torah is not only the axis of the liturgy, the organ of the ritual, it is finally the irreducible basis of all authentic Jewish thought. It is quite remarkable that the Oral Law, that collection of rabbinical traditions of a juridical, doctrinal, or philosophical nature, is as a whole attributed to Moses just as much as the written Law, the Pentateuch. The fact that this Oral Law was itself finally written down, is considered by the Jews as merely accidental, as something imposed by historical

Jew from Warsaw saving the Torah (*Maurice Mendjisky*)

exigencies which should by no means detract from its fundamentally oral character. For in Jewish thought the idea of the Oral Law signifies above all else the vitality of the Written Law. Elsewhere the Letter and the Spoken Word are at variance; they are mutually exclusive or, at best, complementary. In Judaism they are organically united in an inseparable whole. In each letter there lies hidden the power of the spoken word; in each spoken word a literal sign. This idea has created a completely original domain, which no Jew can enter without feeling he has discovered his spiritual home; which no Jew can leave without feeling he has lost his home. I mean the domain of *study*. You must not take it as an intellectual pursuit, as something only accessible to the privileged; you must give it an emotional and popular connotation. You might imagine a university where the tasks of everyday life, of thought, and of action are studied. When you have done this, you will have an inkling of what the Jew feels, who attends one of the innumerable large or small schools, or, simpler still, who retires alone or with a few friends to a corner of his house to *study* the Torah. There he is perpetually apprenticed to his half real, half prophetic life and to that history which is as indissolubly literal and inspired as the Torah he is studying.

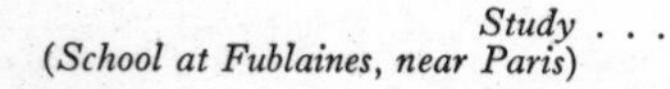

Study . . .
(*School at Fublaines, near Paris*)

It is even more remarkable, however, that Jewish mysticism should have developed on the basis of the text of the Torah. For the very hallmark of mysticism is that it goes beyond the letter, the word, and even the spoken word in order to reach the Ineffable. 'Whatever cannot be expressed in words' is dear to the soul of the mystic. Now Jewish mysticism has this peculiarity that it exhausts the meaning of each word. The Zohar is a commentary of the Torah. It comments upon its words, one by one, or rather letter by letter, sign by sign, yet in doing so it works its way into the depths of an intense and luminous spirituality, and rises to sublime approaches to God. In the eighteenth century East European Judaism was on the verge of dividing into two groups: the *Mitnagdim* rationalists, and the new adepts of *Hassidism.* If the break had taken place, one factor would have safeguarded the spiritual cohesion of the people: the fundamental writings of both movements, the Talmud and the Zohar, are both commentaries on the text of the Torah.

We have already indicated that the commentaries on the text are not simple repetitions. In Judaism the range of spiritual subjects and philosophical theories amplifying the text of the Torah is very wide. And sometimes you gain the impression that you have strayed far from Moses and the sense he himself

. . . and prayer
(Hostel for the Young at Strasbourg)

gave to the Law. Does not the relationship with the Oral Law, as it is specified in the Talmud, jump several important links? 'Moses was initiated into the Torah from Sinai onwards. He transmitted it to Joshua; Joshua to the Elders; the Elders transmitted it to the Prophets; and the Prophets transmitted it to the men of the Great Synagogue' (*Mishnah Abot*, 1: 1). Where are the priests? the kings? Some were unworthy, others pious. This Pharisaical approach to the history of the Torah is characteristic: it only retains the democratic and prophetical links, relegating the sacerdotal and institutional elements to the margin. Yet these also have their place in the development of Judaism. There are numerous attempts to sublimate all those passages in the Torah dealing with the priesthood, with sacrifices, and with the Temple. If Philo platonized in this field, many rabbis have philonized. The system of Maimonides, a worthy precursor to St Thomas Aquinas, who quotes and eulogizes it, has all the faults and qualities of the medieval *summae*. The disciples of Moses Maimonides will say: 'Between Moses and Moses, there has been none like Moses.' Nevertheless, by interpreting certain passages of the Torah in a therapeutic or hygienic sense, the work of the second Moses hides much of the work of the first. And Moses Mendelssohn, this third Moses who later shared the praises accorded to the former two, forgets, as Jewish philosophers of the nineteenth century will forget after him, that the imperatives of the Torah of Moses have not a Kantian category at their source, but the will of a personal God.

Such examples might be multiplied. And from mere apologetical vanity it might be emphasized that their number proves the 'spiritual tolerance' of Judaism and its 'readiness to absorb outside influences'. As a matter of fact, these Jews were animated by something far more absolute than mere tolerance: they were animated by the authentic Mosaic conviction that they were 'bearing the yoke of the Kingdom'. For if faithfulness to the text of the Torah is the soul of Judaism, faithfulness to the *act* of the Torah is its heart. Beyond or, rather, in the centre of the most subtle and sometimes most remote interpretations of the letter of the word of Moses, there lay the acceptance of the *act* commanded by Moses. This acceptance did not take refuge in any allegorical or symbolical explanations, but consisted in the literal performance of the act, of the *Mitzvah*.

In order to realize the full implication of the word *Mitzvah*, as of the word *Torah*, we must be familiar with the term 'faithfulness to Moses'.

In order to understand the nature of a *Mitzvah*, you must have performed one. For the outside observer it is a matter of making a gesture, performing a rite, the mechanical performance of which betrays an empty formalism. Mere obedience to the letter is not unfamiliar to the Jew, and no one is more contemptuous of it than he. The most violent antagonists of all false Pharisaism are the Pharisees themselves. Some pages of the Talmud condemn formalism even more emphatically than do the Gospels. But when the Jewish Pharisee judges the act from within, from the very heart of its performance, he has an experience in which all ideas of 'form', 'content' and 'mechanism' have lost their meaning. For all these terms were coined in Greece, a thousand years after Moses; and for him form and content are one in the act of the Torah, in the *Mitzvah*. For him, further, a human act could in no wise be conceived as being in the likeness of a machine, for it is essentially in the likeness of God.

For the Jew, therefore, performing a *Mitzvah* means accepting once again the Torah of Moses in its full literal and organic sense. It means rejecting with Moses the dichotomy between spirit and flesh, and by holiness restoring the unity of man who was created in the likeness of the unity of God. In this effort to achieve unity the commandments of the Torah soften their imperative character in favour of the imitative and, above all, in favour of participation. The *yoke* is not arbitrarily laid on an unwilling neck. It is accepted freely and gladly in the realization that on this acceptance or this refusal the fate of the Kingdom of God on earth depends. This sole reliance on the *redemptive* efficaciousness of the *Mitzvah* explains the great break that took place between Judaism and Christianity at the time of St

Paul. The tension between Faith and the Law would never have led to the schism, had the choice only been between legalism and true spirituality. Since Moses, since Abraham, nay since Adam, Jewish 'orthodoxy' has known that the Law is quickened by the Word, that it implies an inner spiritual life without which it would only be a parody of the Will of God. The parallelism in the contemporary teaching of Hillel the Pharisee, and Jesus whom the Pharisees addressed as *Rabbi*, with the respect due to the master, shows that the Sermon on the Mount is in the authentic Pharisaic tradition of Judaism. But the Apostle Paul poses the problem of *justification*: justification by the redemptive Law, or justification by faith in a Redeemer? By thus placing the dialectic of Faith and the Law within the framework of redemption, St Paul gave rise to the schism. For the Jews it was not the Messiah who justified man, but the *Mitzvah*, the fulfilment of the Law. At all times and in all places, the Kingdom of God on earth was inaugurated *within the four cubits of the fulfilment of the Torah.* Four cubits is a small space: yet it can contain a man who takes upon himself the yoke of the Kingdom.

A bulky anthology would not suffice to assemble all the texts in mystical and talmudical literature describing the *messianic* power of the Torah. However, a distinction must be made between those texts that lay emphasis on the Torah itself, and those others which ascribe all messianic efficaciousness to the man who fulfils the Torah, to the man in the *Mitzvah.* At the very heart of Judaism there is an externalized and spectacular conception of the Torah. In the eyes of some Jews the Torah, hypostatized and expanded to cosmic dimensions, fulfils all the functions elsewhere attributed to Wisdom, to the Logos, to the Messiah. Before all creation the Torah allowed God to create the universe, being at the same time its plan and framework, its building and consummation. Yet there is also an inner conception of the Torah through the *Mitzvah*: it is the man who fulfils the Torah, within whose four cubits all cosmic efficaciousness is contained. He is needed by God to continue the work of creation, to plan, to carpenter, to build, and to complete the universe. The very coexistence of these two conceptions has

Rabbi at prayer (*Chagall*)

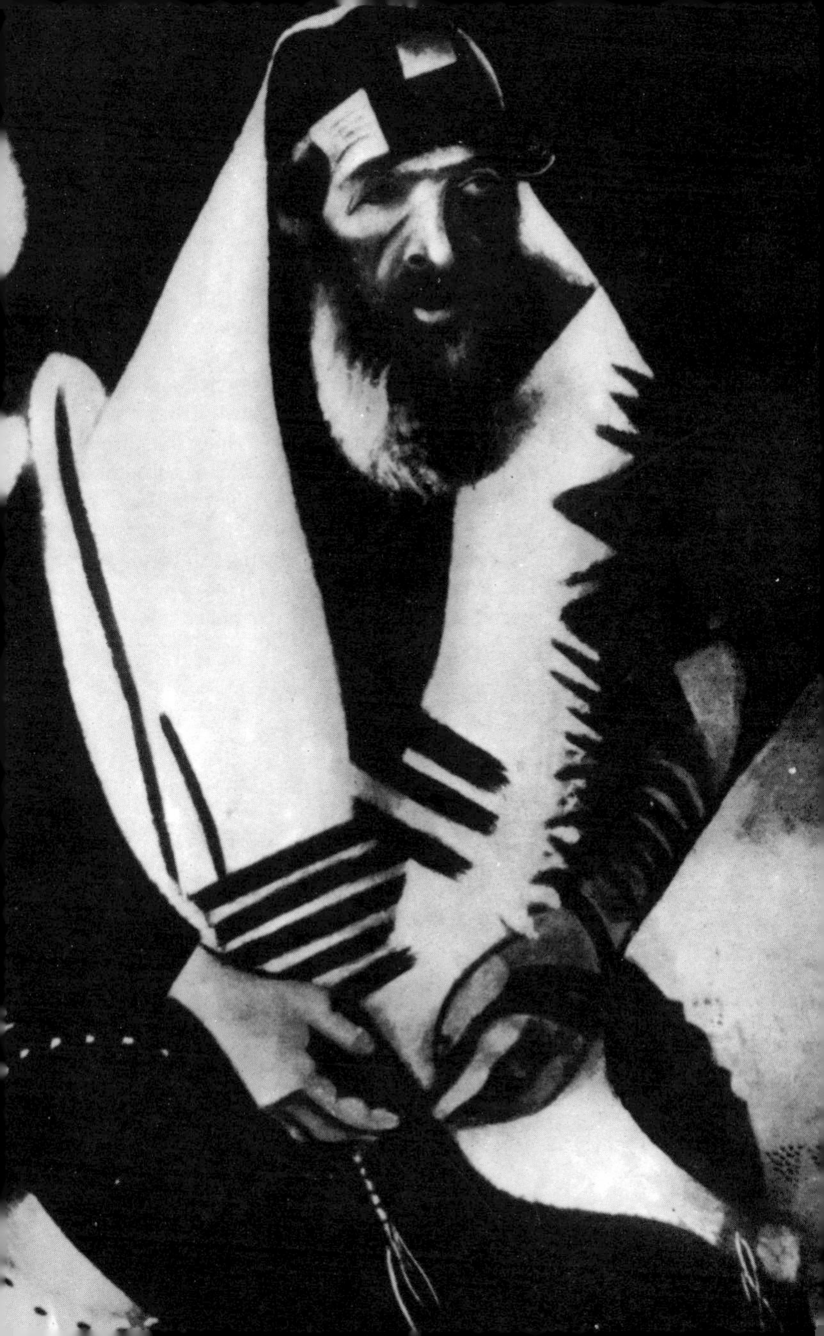

enabled Judaism to differentiate itself from Christianity until this very day. Yet it must be recognized that, especially in our day, there are Jews who are content to *speak* differently about the Messiah to the Christian, while there are other Jews for whom the difference between the Jew and the Christian lies, in the last resort, not only on the level of the spoken word, but on that of the messianic *act*.

These latter find an even deeper meaning in their fidelity to Moses. They know that if the Torah in itself is the Law of the universe, the fulfilment of the Torah is nevertheless entrusted to the Jewish people alone: it is they who are challenged. The Law does not build up the world by seizing it indiscriminately at every angle with all its might: it seeks to fulfil itself through the narrow Jewish medium. The path of God leads through the four cubits of the *Mitzvah*. At each stage, when the Jew, who is challenged, fulfils the Law, and only then, the Law receives the impetus towards a more universal realization. This does not depend only on the perpetuation of the event of Sinai in the centre of the Jewish vocation. The permanence of the experience of the desert is also essential.

THE COVENANT: THE LONELINESS OF THE MESSIANIC CALLING

> *Lo, it is a people that dwells alone,*
> *And shall not be reckoned among the nations.*
> (Num. 23: 9)

It is Balaam, an inspired non-Jew, who in the account of Moses throws light on the quintessence of the Jewish people. A minimum of inspiration and of acceptance of the world of the Bible is indeed necessary to the understanding of the solitude of Israel. The mere spectator who refuses to accept the point of view of the Bible, will regard this solitude simply as Jewish particularism or cosmopolitanism with its apparent and so irritating and harmful arrogance that seems to disturb the order of things without rhyme or reason. Haman the Agagite defines this in the following words:

> There is a certain people scattered abroad and dispersed among the peoples in all the provinces of thy kingdom; and their laws are diverse from those of every people; neither keep they the king's laws: therefore it is not for the king's profit to suffer them. If it please the king, let it be written that they be destroyed (Esther 3: 8–9).

That is the programme of the anti-semite whom the Jew meets on his way throughout the centuries. This programme rests on a fundamental misinterpretation, a ridiculous view of reality. For Jewish particularism does not give rise to a 'Jewish question': it raises a problem. The election of Israel is not a caprice; it is a mystery. 'In vain does Dostoevski present Russia as a chosen nation; in vain does Péguy take pleasure in claiming the same distinction for France; in vain does "British Israel" multiply its pseudo-exegetic proofs to show that they are members of the Ten Lost Tribes; in vain do Christians from all countries cover their meditations on the destiny of the Jews with all the dust of our infidelities and the doubtful varnish of our imaginings: not even the arguments of "Christian" sociology, not even "independent" historical discoveries, not even "philosemitical" moral or psychological fluctuations in Christian feeling can ever allow us to forget that even today Israel is the only people whose name can be qualified by the epithet "mystery" without committing a sacrilege. Take it or leave it' (F. Lovsky, *Le Mystère d'Israël et l'antisémitisme*).

Let us then accept what is offered by the generosity and intelligence of F. Lovsky. Before him others have pondered the mystery of Israel. Yet his book, which is one of the most recent in the French language, surpasses its predecessors by its wealth of information and the vigour of its research. As Jews we can repeat with this clearsighted Christian that the Jewish people do not consider their wanderings a curse. The nomadism of Israel is not that of Cain. The exile of the Jewish people is not an aimless, unsettled wandering. Only the parody of the Wandering Jew bears the stigma of infamy. We can also repeat with Lovsky that if the Jewish people consider their wanderings as a chastisement, it is because they accept the significance of the trial in the light of their meditations on the lesson of Job, and prefer to justify God rather than themselves. This preference gives no adversary (and even less a friend, *vide* Job) the right to constitute himself as the interpreter of the designs of God, as his mouthpiece in the process, as his secular arm, or even worse as his well-meaning *claque*, the hired clappers who applaud the show

The Wandering Jew (Picture from Épinal)

and then go and have dinner. We must, however, leave Lovsky before he draws his conclusions: the claims of authenticity force us as well as him to explore the 'mystery' from our proper point of view. Here the inescapable ambiguousness of the Judaeo-Christian dialogue manifests itself. The hyphen unites the two terms; but it also breaks them asunder. However necessary it may be to insist on its unifying nature, it is equally indispensable, at certain stages of the analysis, to accept its power of separation. For the Jew the 'mystery' of the election of Israel has a significance which Christianity cannot contain. Where is its source? Plainly speaking, it does not lie in Jesus, but in Moses; not on Golgotha, where the New Covenant of the Christians was made, but in the desert, where the Old Covenant was born, the only one the Jews acknowledge. It was the desert which Moses had caught sight of and lived through; a desert which is not a place of isolation, but of an encounter; where men are not petrified in the immobility of a hermitage, but where a whole people faced their historical destiny. In spite of the limits set it in time and in space—forty years between the Nile Delta and the Jordan—the adventure in the desert remained incompleted in time and in space. As a matter of fact a third dimension, that of the Covenant, encloses it on all sides, projecting the adventure outside the *hic et nunc* on to other ages and other spaces. The march through the desert was certainly the route to the Promised Land; yet the land did not realize the promise in a definite manner. It was prepared to receive a people, but equally to 'spew it out', if it broke the Covenant; and then to receive it again, if it again 'sought the Covenant with all its heart and all its soul'.

Later ages of history and other lands than the land of Canaan already gravitate towards the desert, where Moses and Israel experience an adventure, which has the nature of an axis. For round this desert, where a people who are 'not like the others' advance towards a Land which is 'not like the others', a whole universe develops, as round its central axis. Such is the 'mystery' of this singularity of the desert. Paradoxically it makes the solitary people into a companion throughout the ages; it makes the Promised Land into the companion of all lands. In the desert of her particular existence Israel meets the universal. 'Ye shall be unto me a nation of priests and a holy people, for all the earth is Mine. Among all the peoples ye shall be a treasure.' Since the desert, the earth and its peoples are no longer shapeless masses, without colour or direction. From henceforth they are lines orientated with regard to an axis, which is the axis of God. Since the desert Israel knows that she is in the centre of a cosmography where each people has its characteristic function. Egypt is the host-nation with all the terrible ambiguity of the term, for the host can assassinate as well as welcome the stranger sheltering under his roof (Deut. 8–9). Edom is the brother-nation, but did not Cain slay his brother (Deut. 23: 7; Num. 20: 18)? Ammon and Moab are neutral nations, but is not neutrality worse than hatred in certain circumstances (Deut. 23: 3–6)? Midian is the nation of beguiling beauty; but beauty can corrupt the soul (Num. 25: 1–19).

The thought of the prophets cannot be understood unless the theme of the desert is seen from this angle of Moses. The problem which troubled Amos, Hosea, Jeremiah and Ezekiel, who untiringly evoked the desert, is not a cultural but a religious one; it is not moral, but metaphysical. We must not confound prophethood with Rechabitism. The Rechabites, who formed a nomad sect in the ninth century during the reign of Ahab and Jezebel, were reacting against the excesses of an impure civilization. For them the desert was an object of nostalgia. They withdrew into it in order to recapture the simplicity of a golden age, realized in the distant past.

The ascetic nomadism of Biblical times is crystallized around them as well as certain of their predecessors and followers (among whom Jean Steinmann rightly numbers the Essenes and St John the Baptist). However, in spite of certain affinities in temperament, the prophets consider the desert in quite a different light from the Rechabites, even in a light that is directly opposed to that of the Rechabites or Essenes. The latter, as a matter of fact, in their flight from civilization, are at the same time fleeing from life on the historical plane. The desert places them in the margin of the historical life of the Jewish people. And it is a remarkable thing that the Essenes, despite the fact that their doctrine is at all points in conformity with Jewish orthodoxy, even intensifying it, should not have survived within the Jewish people. This is because they had renounced something that the prophets considered essential to the experience of the desert: the intimate and indestructible connection between Jewish history and Jewish religion. For the prophets' return to the desert did not merely mean the restoration of the purity of the heart, but the restoration of sacred history. When history is faced with a blank wall, when it meets failure, then the desert provides a way of escape from the impasse, and enables man to emerge victorious. Hosea and Jeremiah express this in the symbolic language of matrimony: in the desert, where formerly the espousals between God and Israel took place, the married couple, violently separated by cruel treachery, will unite once more in the ardent desire to renew their common life. Literally repeating the terms used in the sacred cosmography of the Pentateuch, Ezekiel evokes the 'desert of the peoples'. In this desert, which is by no means exotic or of secondary importance, but set in the midst of all nations, Israel will once more find itself inexorably face to face with God. Then she will understand the meaning of her election, of her 'not being like the others' in the heart of the Kingdom of God:

> And that which cometh into your mind shall not be at all; in that ye say, We will be as the nations, as the families of the countries, to serve wood and stone. As I live, saith the Lord God, surely with a mighty hand, and with a stretched out arm, and with fury poured out, will I be king over you: and I will bring you out from the peoples, and will gather you out of the countries wherein ye are scattered, with a mighty hand, and with a stretched out arm, and with fury poured out: and I will bring you into the wilderness of the peoples, and there will I plead with you face to face. Like as I pleaded with your fathers in the wilderness of the land of Egypt, so I will plead with you, saith the Lord God (Ezek. 20: 32–6).

It is interesting to note that the prophets not only interpreted the idea of the desert in the sense Moses attached to it, but also the rite expressing this idea in the Pentateuch. If the Passover actually restores the moment of the Exodus from Egypt in a ritual manner, the march across the desert is repeated in the feast of Sukkoth (Lev. 23: 33–44). Each year for seven days the Jews symbolically leave their solid 'man-made' houses and shelter under leaves and branches in the open air, thus restoring the fullness of nomad life.

Nomad, or rather human. For though it is not to be denied that from ancient times the feast of Sukkoth was celebrated in the definite desire not to renounce the values of nomad life for good, it is no less characteristic that the historical significance of the desert was very early associated with it. If there is a prophet for whom the central position of Israel and Jerusalem is one of the fundamental realities of history, it is certainly Zechariah: 'Yea, many peoples and strong nations shall come to seek the Lord of hosts in Jerusalem. . . . In those days it shall come to pass, that ten men shall take hold, out of all the languages of the nations, shall even take hold of the skirt of him that is a Jew, saying, We will go with you, for we have heard that God is with you' (Zech. 8: 22–3). In the fourteenth chapter of his prophecy Zechariah expands this gravitation round the Jew to the measure of a cosmic eschatology, and he localizes its internal principles in the rites of the feast of Sukkoth. It is this feast, the final resurrection of the march across the desert of Egypt, that will receive not only individuals, but nations; not only those who wish to pray, but those who hunger after life. And the Talmud also knows that the seventy bulls, the sacrifice of which at the feast of Sukkoth is prescribed by Leviticus, symbolize the presence of the seventy nations of the earth in the very centre of all religion, in the Temple of Jerusalem. Rabbi Johanan says: 'Had

The sack of the Temple by Titus

the nations understood the significance of the Temple, they would not have destroyed it, but built it with their own hands, for the sacrifice, offered there, was for them.

There is no rite which shows the sacramental insertion of the Chosen People into a framework of universal scope more forcibly than the feast of Tabernacles. If the consciousness Israel possesses of her special election may be described as *Paschal*, it may be said that the universal nature of this election is *Sukkothic*.

During the period of the Talmud, Jewish thought, when considering the mystery of Israel, is concerned with the study of the historical desert, which had already been powerfully expounded by the prophets. The period of the Talmud was the time of exile, when the Jewish people were scattered all over the globe. Even now Judaism has not yet emerged from this dramatic situation; and though it is true that times have changed, that the Talmudic period was followed by the age of medieval philosophy, then by the mystical Renaissance, and finally by the modern age of emancipation; yet the spiritual interpretation of the elements of the drama remains identical with the one propounded by the eye-witnesses of the fall of the Temple, and the destruction of the Jewish state by Vespasian and Titus in the year 70.

The beginning of the Exile was not an unexpected catastrophe for its Jewish contemporaries. They were not suddenly faced with it without any spiritual preparation. The event only overwhelmed those Jews who had denied the 'secret' of their history. Among these were the Sadducees, who identified the history of Israel with the Temple and the State: concrete, but petrified institutions; the Essenes, who had left the domain of history in order to live on its borders in an eternity of contemplation; the Ebionites or Judaeo-Christians, holding that human history had come to an end with Jesus, and yet forced to acknowledge that history went on all the same. The catastrophe swept the ground from under the feet of these realists, these escapists, and these perplexed men. They could not understand its significance. But the mass of the Jewish people, the Pharisees

Moses and the Shekinah, by Krol

of Palestine and all those who had been living in the Babylonian or Mediterranean diaspora for centuries, had their fate enlightened by the 'secret' of their history, whose depositories and faithful associates they felt they were. They brought the scattering of the Chosen People over all the nations into line with the sacred cosmography of the Torah of Moses, this Exile into a feast of Sukkoth, extended in time and in space, calling for a new march through the desert of the nations. This vocation to an exile, the ends of which were not known, but which the Jews were prepared to face to the very end, would not have been accepted with such alacrity unless from the very outset one of the themes of the desert had been pondered with extraordinary intensity: the theme of the *Shekinah*.

This Hebrew term, which is an original creation of Pharisaic thought, cannot be found before the Talmud in any of the innumerable Jewish, apocalyptic, Hellenistic or Essenian texts, all of which abound in theological terms. Nor is it found in the

Bible. Yet its origins are undeniably Biblical. We must go very far back to find them, as far back as the desert where the dwelling place of God is designated by the Hebrew root *shakhan*, of which *Shekinah* is a simple derivative. In Pharisaic spirituality *Shekinah* means *God-in-Exile*. Thus the *Revelation* which is confirmed by the dwelling place or *residence* was nothing else but a divine exile. Actually for both the Revelation and the Exile the same Biblical root is used (*galôh*). God's sojourn in the desert in the midst of the people of Israel was a Divine Exile, a dwelling under the Tabernacle among the Hebrews, who were also sheltered by the Tabernacle. The human adventure was accompanied by a divine. This adventure recommences from the first moment of the dispersion. Israel goes into exile. God goes with her. The *Shekinah* is the companion of Israel in the desert of the nations. A new *Revelation* begins. The *Exile* and the *Revelation* are announced simultaneously.

The fruitfulness and the scope of this idea can be easily surmised. The *Shekinah* resides with every exiled fragment of the Jewish people. In every particle of land trodden by a Jew in exile the presence of God is revealed. Far from being an outward road leading the Chosen People farther and farther away from the centre of their election, the Exile is for Israel a mission, each stage of which strengthens the bonds between the Jew and the God who accompanies him. It is a mission of the heart; for the universe would be lacking in shape unless Israel were omnipresent, making the Divine sap pulsate through the organism of the cosmos like blood through the body. It is a mission of maintaining God's time; for on the dial of the centuries, each of which marks a different human hour, Israel alone marks the permanent hour of God. Finally it is a mission of *Redemption*; for every land that is reached by the Jew in Exile is also reached by the God who accompanies him; and thus in each field of his Exile the Jew places the seeds, which will one day all together bring forth the Divine harvest throughout the whole earth. The texts which we shall quote later give an idea of the diversity of the missionary spirit in the Exile, which has been pondered and pondered by the Jews of all ages and all varieties of opinion. French

Martyred Jew, by Chagall

readers are offered a magnificent anthology, collected by the pupils of Jacob Gordin, in the *Notes sur la Galout* (in *Aspects du Génie d'Israël*, Cahiers du Sud, 1950).

This redemptive aspect of the sufferings of Israel in Exile may evoke many parallels in the mind of the Christian; it may attribute to the Jewish people much of what, in the Christian dispensation, derives from Jesus; this spiritual concordance may be completed by a further concretely historical one, namely 'that the sufferings of Israel have more and more distinctly assumed the shape of the Cross' (Jacques Maritain, *Raison et Raisons*). These are questions that concern the Christian. For the Jew the sources of this dispensation are Biblical. Does not an uninterrupted Jewish exegesis, which goes far beyond the Christian era, see in the Suffering Servant of the fifty-third chapter of Isaiah the figure of the Jewish people? But above all, the desert is there in the Torah, offering the *types* in which the Jewish people rightly recognize their own destiny.

It is not only the theme of the *Shekinah* that Jewish thought has gleaned from the desert, but others as well which all cooperate in throwing light on the 'mystery' of Israel. Together with the *Shekinah* the Jewish people are engaged in the adventure of the redemption. But the way is beset with dangers. Violence and cunning lie in wait at every crossroad. Who is this brutal, wily enemy that, in barring the road to Israel, bars it at the same time to humanity and to God? Who is this anti-Jew who claims that there is nothing mysterious or metaphysical in the destiny of Israel, and who in each century asserts that there is a definitive solution to the Jewish question? Jewish thought calls him Amalek. Of this Amalek the Nebuchadnezzars, the Hamans, Titus, Torquemada, Chmielnicki, and the Hitlers of all time are only reincarnations. For Amalek was the people who were the first in the desert to molest Israel (or, according to a more accurate translation, to rob her of the halo granted by Providence) (Exod. 17: 8–16; Deut. 25: 17–19); they were the people against whom Moses declared a perpetual war (according to the traditional interpretation of Exod. 17: 16; for as long as they are there the Divine Name and the Divine Throne are destroyed). It is remarkable that the Jewish typology of Good and Evil should not have chosen God and Satan as antagonistic but the *Shekinah* and Amalek, whose first encounter took place in the desert.

However, beyond Good and Evil, the experience of the desert still nourishes the mysterious Exile of the Jewish people. As the march through the desert was directed towards the Land, the eschatology of the Exile is directed towards the Land. The Exile and the Land are bound by a dialectic which is not merely of the intellectual order. The most dramatic events in the Jewish history of the dispersion bear witness to the existential value of this dialectic. In the desert there were faint-hearted men who were afraid of conquering, and died in despair in the desert, while the valiant reached the Land. In the desert there were also die-hards who risked the attack, even without God, even against God, provided it was against Amalek (Num. 14: 44–5). And there were the patient souls who awaited the signal of God. Likewise, in the desert of the Exile events, which were messianically decisive, divided the camp of Israel between those who loved the Exile and those who loved the Land.

This was the case with the false Messiahs, who have arisen periodically in Jewish history: Bar Kocheba, David Reubeni, Sabbatai Zevi and many others. In our day we have the

eschatological significance of the Zionist movement and the re-establishment of the State of Israel, which can only be understood in the light of this dialectic of the desert. No doubt, as Bialik pointed out from the very inception of Zionism, the message of Herzl meant to break with the 'Dead of the Desert', with the apathetic victims of a fate suffered meaninglessly in Egypt, in Spain, in Poland, in Kishinev (soon it will come to Auschwitz). It summoned the Jews to form the first exilic generation to live and be victorious. However, life and death are not the only two things to choose from. The problem is not solely one of the suicide or survival of a people. It is the problem of the success or failure of a mission. The first Zionist pioneers were above all die-hards. Without God they cleared the Holy Land, while the majority of the faithful were awaiting a signal from God. Today both groups work together in the Holy Land, and they feel strongly that they are accomplishing a missionary task. Nevertheless they accuse those who are still in the dispersion of betraying their vocation by refusing the Land. In reality those who refuse are no traitors, provided that their refusal does not arise from selfishness or love of ease, but from the consciousness of their situation as exiles. The State of Israel and the Diaspora form the two branches in the dialectic of messianic Judaism. The Jewish people have constantly to choose between Faith and Hope. Those who believe have more courage; those who hope are stronger. It is again the situation of the desert. But it also teaches the Jew that, in order to embark on the one way or the other, he may not wait till he finds out which of the two will lead to the goal. This direct challenge, this choice which must be made here and now for all eternity, gives the 'Mystery' of Israel its radiance. This is what Judah ha Levi and after him Rabbi Isaac Levi of Berdichev have called 'the joy of the Exile'. And by its roots in the situation of the desert, it is identical with 'the joy of the Messiah'.

The Faith kept by the Jewish People with Moses: Seven Trends

1. *THE PASCHAL MEAL FOR MEN*

For Judaism the central subject of the Exodus is proclaimed in the liturgical lesson for the last day of the Octave of the Passover: the chapter dealing with the universal messianic peace:

> And the wolf shall dwell with the lamb, and the leopard shall lie down with the kid; and the calf and the young lion and the fatling together; and a little child shall lead them. And the cow and the bear shall feed; their young ones shall lie down together; and the lion shall eat straw like the ox. And the sucking child shall play on the hole of the asp, and the weaned child shall put his hand on the basilisk's den. They shall not hurt nor destroy in all my holy mountain: for the earth shall be full of the knowledge of the Lord, as the waters cover the sea (Isaiah 11:6–9).

Here is 'the dream of the wandering Jew' as it is crystallized in the night of the Passover by the great contemporary Jewish poet, Edmond Fleg:

> Awake, awake! Behold and see!
> On all the peaks, on all the plains,
> In closed valleys, open gulfs,
> On all the seas and archipelagos
> The table for mankind is laid!
>
> And on the table made of wood, from every wood,
> A napkin that is spread for all,
> Woven with all the fires that flow down from all
> the skies.
> The cover is laid, the cups are blessed,
> Creation all around communicates,

And here—among the beasts
That far outnumber
All mankind, the Wolf walks with the Lamb,
Making the Peace of the World!

Behold, they are come, their naked bodies tinted,
The men whose lips are black . . .

And see here, squatting quite close to them
The men whose skulls are red . . .

And here, from out their distant world
The men whose skulls are yellow . . .

And here—now come the men with white fore-
heads . . .

Arise, arise! Your place is empty in their midst,
Their faces shine with happiness
All round that immense table!
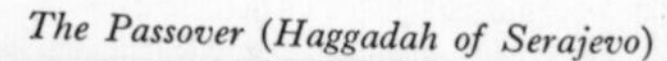
Behold, they have broken the Bread!
Behold, they have raised the Wine!
Listen, they have prayed in the silence:

The Holy Supper of Mankind begins!

The Passover (*Haggadah of Serajevo*)

2. *THE LITERAL WORD OF THE BIBLE*

Preliminary note: The Jewish reading of the Bible can be varied. Here are three interpretations of a verse which might seem fairly barren, ritualistic, and old-fashioned. Yet, in spite of the remarkable diversity in their approach, rationalistic, mystical, and historical, they penetrate the Divine secret contained in the text.

And whether it be cow or ewe, ye shall not kill it and her young both in one day (Lev. 22: 28).

It was forbidden to sacrifice the mother with her young so that we might take heed not to strangle the little one before the eyes of its mother; for in this case the animal would experience too great a pain. As a matter of fact, in this respect there is no difference in the degree of pain experienced by a man and other animals. For the love and tenderness a mother has for her child does not depend on reason, but on the workings of the imagination, which the majority of animals possess as well as man. . . . If the Torah has been mindful of such distress of soul in animals, what must its attitude be with regard to men? (Moses Maimonides, *Guide of the Perplexed*, III, 48; 12th century)

The motive of this prohibition cannot have been the anxiety to spare an animal moral pain. If that had been so, it would have sufficed for the Torah to have prescribed that the mother and its young be sacrificed apart, the one in one place the other in another. However, this prohibition does not affect space but time, the indivisible 'day', which is at the same time terrestrial and celestial. Here every act of cruelty, whatsoever its nature, makes an irreparable breach. The unity of this 'day' at which God and men are working together can only be safeguarded by an act of love. (Zohar, Commentary on the above verse; 12th century)

When at the destruction of the Temple convoys of hungry, thirsty, tortured Jews were dragging themselves in chains along the road to Babylon to disappear or be assassinated, Moses arose and said unto God: 'Master of the world! Thou hast written in the Torah: "And whether it be cow or ewe, ye shall not kill it and her young both in one day." And now, how many Jewish children have already been sacrificed with their mothers . . . and Thou art silent!' (Midrach Rabba, *On the Book of Lamentations*, Introduction; 5th century)

Fundamental note: All the same, the Jewish interpretation of the Bible is unvaryingly prepared to renounce all interpretations of any kind, since, for the Jew, the Spirit of the verse lies in the act which it evokes. On this question both the medieval philosopher and the twentieth-century thinker are agreed.

Human reason is out of place in matters of divine action, on account of its incapacity to grasp them. Reason must rather obey, just as a sick person must obey the physician in applying his medicines and advice. Consider how little circumcision has to do with philosophy, and how small is its social influence.

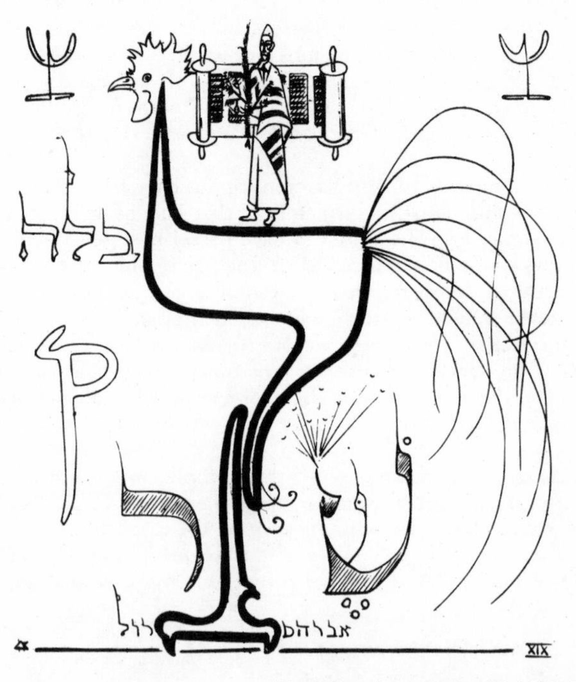

The Hebrew letter Q, the initial of Qabbala, is mystical letter par excellence: it is also the init of the name of the artist in Hebrew transcripti Qrol (Abraham Krol, Homage to Scripture)

Yet Abraham, in spite of the hardship the very nature of this command must have seemed at his age, subjected his person and children to it, and it became the sign of the covenant, of the attachment of the Divine Influence to him. (Jehuda ha Levi, *Kuzari* 3: 7; beginning of 12th century)

Is, perhaps, the content of the Bible, the manner in which the will of God was made known to man, symbolic? Do we pray symbolically? Do we implore Him for symbolic aid? . . .

He who loves with all his heart, with all his soul, with all his might, does not love symbolically. Nor does the term 'to serve God' refer to a symbolic attitude. The symbolists claim that it is not the literal meaning of Scripture that is the important matter but rather the spiritual truths hidden beneath it; while Jewish tradition insists that the Biblical commandment be not divested of *peshat*, of its naked meaning; without the reality of the naked word the spirit is a ghost. Even the mystics who cherished the allegorical meaning of Scripture and regarded the hidden significance as superior to the plain, naked meaning, always insisted that the secret rests upon the plain. . . . Religious observance has more than two dimensions; it is more than an act that happens between man and an idea. . . . In a religious act man stands before God. (Abraham Heschel, *Man's Quest for God*, New York, 1954)

3. *THE IMMEDIACY OF GOD*

If we wish to centre this subject like the preceding ones around the figure of Moses, we should be hard put to it to find a single text as an illustration. This is obvious. For a single word in Jewish literature, suggesting that Moses were other than one man among many, would rob the subject of all its meaning.

In the world of the Jew the encounter between God and men is indeed immediate. Even Moses, the supreme prophet, neither tried, nor wished, nor was able to place himself between God and men.

Hence this impressive silence in Jewish liturgy, which is more decisive than whole catalogues mentioning his name. In the supreme moments of the liturgy the Synagogue deliberately excludes the name of Moses in order that pious veneration should not make this 'modest' man, who nevertheless reached the limits of what is possible to human nature, into a superman or a mediator.

The Synagogue says: God of Abraham, God of Isaac, God of Jacob. She never says: God of Moses.

The Synagogue does not say: Moses delivered us from Egypt, but God alone. In the Passover Haggadah the name of Moses is not even mentioned.

'Moses died, who would not die?' This is the conclusion of a liturgical elegy which places Moses by the side of all men, thus allowing them to meet God face to face.

Moses, Miriam and the people, singing the hymn of thanksgiving

4. *INTIMACY WITH GOD*

To his intimacy with God, the Jew brings not only the familiar note of an old experience, but also the urgent tone of one who knows that he is speaking to the Living God: he says directly 'you' to God. Did not God in the Torah use the familiar term to Israel, when He demanded from her that she should respect His Word for ever? And You God, what do you expect from those who should respect your Word? The Hassidic Rabbi of Berdichev (18th century) replies: Here and now, four cubits tall, and at this very moment of my Jewish existence, I am expecting Redemption:

The Synagogue: the place of the immediate encounter between God and men, between the parents and the children whom they bless (Haggadah of Serajevo)

Good morning, Master of the Universe.
I, Levi Isaac, son of Sara, from Berdichev,
Come into Your presence, to plead:
I represent Your people Israel.
What is the relation between You and Israel?
On every occasion it is said,
'Thus shalt thou say unto the children of Israel!'
On every occasion it is said:
'Speak unto the children of Israel!'

Father of Mercy, how many peoples are there in the world?
Persians, Babylonians, Romans . . .
What do the Russians say?
Their Czar is *the* Czar.
What do the Germans say?
Their empire is *the* Empire.
And I, Levi Isaac, son of Sara, from Berdichev, I say:
May the Divine Name be exalted and sanctified . . .
And I, Levi Isaac, son of Sara, from Berdichev, I say:
I shall not move from here, here I take my stand,
Until the end come,
Until the end of the Exile come:
Yitgadal veyitqadash Sheme rabba . . .
May the Divine Name be exalted and sanctified. . . .

Alleluia! Praise ye the Lord. Praise, O ye servants of the Lord. Praise the name of the Lord! Beginning of Psalm 113. (Haggadah of Mantua, 16th cent.)

5. *THE EXILE OF GOD*

The religious destiny of man is decided in all its amplitude down here on earth. For down here is not only the dwelling place of man, it is the dwelling place of God. The world of the Covenant is not doubled, it does not transcend itself in order to reach the metaphysical plane. It bears its 'metaphysics' within itself. And as of yore God resided in the midst of His people in the desert, which by that very fact became the centre of the world, thus the Shekinah, during the Exile of Israel, is in the centre of the exiled people.

> The essential residence of the Shekinah is on earth. The seven successive sins committed by Adam, the generation of Enoch, the men of the Flood, the men of the Tower of Babel, the Egyptians at the time of Abraham, the Egyptians and the Sodomites at the time of Moses have caused the Shekinah to mount to the seventh heaven. But the merits of Abraham, Isaac and Jacob, of Levi, Kehat, and Amram, and finally of Moses have brought it back again to the earth. (Talmudic literature, *Pesikta*, 1: 2)

My beloved is mine, and I am His!
He is my God, and I am His people.
He is my Father, and I am His child.
He is my Shepherd, and I am His flock.
He praises me, and I praise Him.
He proclaims my unity, and I proclaim His.
When I am in need of anything,
I demand it of Him,
And when He is in need of anything,
He demands it of me,
For it is said: Speak to the children of Israel,
Say to the children of Israel,
That they do this for Me,
That they do that for Me!
When I am in distress,
I come to Him,
And when He is in distress,
He comes to me,
For it is said: I am with My people in their distress.
(*Midrash*, Rabba on the Song of Songs, 2: 16)

The Shofar of the New Year reminds Israel of her responsibility (13th cent. MS.)

6. *ISRAEL'S TASK OF SUFFERING FOR ALL*

As early as the twelfth century Judah ha Levi writes in his *al Khuzari* (11 : 44) that Israel has a mission of the heart in these centuries of suffering. Israel, the heart of humanity, the suffering servant bears the ills of all, and by this very fact allows God to manifest Himself on earth. Yet, is there still any sense in the isolation of Israel in the centuries of tolerance, emancipation, fraternization? In the nineteenth century Samson Raphael Hirsch answers in the affirmative in a text summing up the non-conformist, for ever prophetical and 'protestant' mission of the Jew.

> Did Judaism ever belong to its age? Can Judaism ever be of its century? Could it have been? Could it become?
>
> Was Abraham a man of his time when the sovereign of his country threw him into the furnace of Chaldaea because he had smashed the idols of his time? Did our ancestors conform to the age when they were forced to be insulted by the Egyptians, to bend their necks under the yoke of slavery for centuries, to let their little ones be buried in the waters of the Nile? Did Daniel conform to his age when, in Babylon together with his young

companions, he was reduced to eat the grass of the fields, preferring to expose his life to the lions rather than to renounce the prayer, which he said three times a day according to the custom of our ancestors, with his face turned towards Jerusalem? Did the Maccabees conform to their age, when they fought the influx of the Greek civilization and its customs with heroic intrepidity? Did the disciples of Hillel and the son of Zakkai conform to their age when the Romans destroyed the kingdom of Judaea with the sword, overthrew the Temple of Jerusalem and led the children of Judah to the slaughter houses or to the slave markets or threw them to the wild beasts as an entertainment for princes? . . . Finally, did this Judaism conform to the age during the centuries, in which our fathers suffered the most infamous oppression, the most insulting scorn, and death in a thousand shapes at all times and in all places? Did Judaism conform to the age during all these centuries? And if Judaism answered the arguments of its contemporaries, did it not run the risk of being misunderstood and misjudged? And was it then an easy thing to be a Jew?—Is Judaism really meant to conform to the age?

What would have happened to Judaism if our fathers had considered it their duty to remodel it according to the spirit of their age? If, in turn, the wisdom of the priests of Meroe in Egypt, the mysteries of Melitta in Babylon, the magic of Zoroaster in Persia, the Eleusinian mysteries or the popular legends of Olympus in Greece, or the fashionable philosophical systems of Alexandria, or Rome the quintessence of all opinions and all beliefs, the teaching of the Druids in Gaul, or the doctrines of the monasteries in the Middle Ages had each time served as standards for the reform of Judaism, and if in our day our fellow Jews were to reform their Judaism by adapting it to the ideas and customs of their compatriots in every country and climate? Do not opinions, customs and needs vary from one country to another, from one century to another? Is not Judaism the religion which is destined, more than any other, to wander through the lands and through the centuries? Should we be obliged to adapt it to one century? . . .

From its beginnings in the Bible it has been clear that Judaism isolates its adherents, that it makes them appear to the superficial observer in each century as though they belonged to a different age. We did not need to discover this fact in modern times. Yet this isolation is only apparent. No religion is more destined to fill its adepts with an all-embracing love than the Jewish religion: it gives them a spirit, a heart to which nothing human in the wide world is alien; it inspires them with the most active and burning sympathy for all human suffering, for all human progress; it makes them hear and acknowledge the Divine footsteps of Eternal Providence in the most obscure paths of history; it makes them plant the banner of hope in the inevitable return to God on the very tomb of a morality which has been totally corrupted. For the whole force of this faith lies in its ability to convince the Jew that all mankind, that all men are marching together with Israel towards the kingdom of God on earth, to a kingdom where truth and love, justice and sanctity will reign everywhere. Look at Abraham, the first Jew on earth. Was any man ever so isolated? He is alone, he is unique, separated from all men, in opposition to his age, to the whole of his age. Yet the heart in his breast is full of modesty and gentleness, full of pity and love for all, even the most corrupt men of his day. The judgement of God is about to strike Sodom and Gomorrha, the most corrupt civilization the world has ever known. And what does Abraham do? He prays for Gomorrha, he prays for Sodom! . . . God has just made a Covenant with him and his descendants, which will isolate him from the rest of the world, and already in the red glow of sunset Abraham is standing outside his tent, waiting for weary wanderers, for strangers and idolators in order to invite them into his dwelling-place, and to show to all men, whatsoever their nature, his pity, his goodness, his all-embracing divine love.

Is there anything surprising in this? This universality, this active love for all humanity, were they not the very essence and the aim, the motif, and the significance of his isolation? Was it not this very universality which isolated Abraham? . . . He remains the symbol of Judaism. Abraham was isolated for the sake of mankind, and for mankind Judaism must continue its lonely march across the ages . . . until the day comes when 'the wolf shall dwell with the lamb, and the leopard shall lie down with the kid: and the calf and the young lion and the fatling together; they shall not hurt nor destroy in all my holy mountain; for the earth shall be full of the knowledge of the Lord, as the waters cover the sea.' Then, and then only: when the age will be with God, Israel will be of its age.

The Visionary (Lithograph by Julienne Hertz)

7. *ISRAEL'S CALLING AND THE REDEMPTION OF THE WORLD*

Jewish mysticism establishes a peculiar connection between the 'God of our Fathers' and 'the Law'. For the general idea of creation it substitutes the idea of a creation in mystery. Here creation itself is mysteriously connected with the Law. The Law is not alien to the world. It provides the key to the mysteries of the world. Behind its obvious words there is a hidden meaning, which expresses the essence of the world. In this way, for the Jew, the book of nature and the starry sky, where men formerly believed they could read the destiny of man in intelligible signs, is replaced by the Book of the Law. This is the central idea of innumerable legends, by means of which Judaism enlarges the apparently narrow limits of its Law so that it can encompass the whole world; on the other hand it sees the future world enclosed in the present since this vision is already pre-figured in the Law. All exegetical methods are employed. . . . Yet the sense of this interpretation, which may appear strange and even ridiculous to the uninitiated, is solely to insert the whole of creation between the God of the Jews and the Jewish Law. Thus God and His Law appear as comprehensive as creation itself.

The idea of the Shekinah establishes a connection between the 'God of our Fathers' and the 'Remnant of Israel'. . . . God gives Himself to this people; he suffers with them; with them he shares the misery of Exile, their wanderings in strange lands. Thus, for the Jew, through the idea that the Torah was created before the world and that the world was created in view of the Torah, the Law has become more than a purely Jewish affair, and can henceforth be considered as part of the foundation of the world. . . . The pride of the 'Remnant of Israel' acquires a more general significance by virtue of the idea of the Shekinah. For the suffering of this remnant, their perpetual separation and segregation now become suffering for God's sake. . . . The idea of an Odyssey of the Shekinah, of the scattering of the Divine spark all over the world, places the whole of revelation between the God of the Jews and the Jew, thus anchoring both God and the remnant in the depths of revelation. In the mysticism of creation merely Jewish concepts have become universal by

The first stages of creation (*Haggadah of Serajevo*)

virtue of the manifold significance of the Law. In the mysticism of revelation the same end is attained by virtue of the profound realization that the Divine suffering involved in God's self-giving to Israel should never have happened, and that by Israel's segregation as a 'remnant' a dwelling-place is provided for the God in exile. This very Divine suffering characterizes the relationship between God and Israel as close, yet still insufficient. God Himself, by 'selling' Himself to Israel and suffering her fate, makes Himself 'needy of redemption'. Thus the relationship between God and the remnant transcends itself in this suffering.

But should not the redemption issue from the relation between the 'remnant' and the 'Law'? How is this relation visualized? What does fulfilling the Law mean to the Jew? What is his conception of it? Why does he do it?

For the sake of a heavenly reward? Do not be like slaves who serve their master because of a reward.

For the sake of earthly satisfaction? Do not say: I do not like pork. Say: I like it very much. But my Father in Heaven has forbidden me to eat it.

No, the Jew fulfils all the innumerable customs and precepts 'in order to unite God and the Shekinah'. With this formula he, the individual, the remnant, prepares his heart 'in fear and love' to fulfil each successive commandment in the name of the whole of Israel. He seeks to gather each separate spark of the glory of God, which is scattered all over the world, from its Exile, and bring it back to Him Who was robbed of it. Each act, each fulfilment of a precept of the Law brings the final unification one step nearer. 'To proclaim the unity of God' is called by the Jew: 'Unifying God'. This unity is no fixed state, it is a slow process. The soul and the hands of man are charged to further this process.

The Jew and the Jewish Law. Between these two limits the drama of redemption, which includes God, the world, and man, is enacted. . . . What is smallest has been enlarged to the measure of the whole, the All; or, rather, it has been redeemed to union with the One. The descent to the innermost depths reveals itself as an ascent to the sublimest heights. What was a purely Jewish sentiment is transfigured into a world-redeeming truth. In the intimate depths of the Jewish heart there shines the Star of Redemption. (Franz Rosenzweig, *Der Stern der Erlösung*, 1921)

NOTE

The translator has made use of the Revised Version of the Bible for quotations from the Pentateuch.

NOTE ON THE ILLUSTRATIONS

SOURCES:

Library of the *Alliance Israélite Universelle*, pp. 2, 18, 26, 34, 36, 38, 40, 42, 44, 46, 89, 90, 126, 128, 134, 145, 151, 163, 168, 172, 173, 174, 180, 184.
Collection of Dr André Bernheim, pp. 7 (b), 8, 9, 10, 13, 14–15, 16, 104, 115, 131, 155.
Photos Izis, pp. 29, 122, 183.
Municipal archives of Strasbourg, pp. 21, 52–3, 62, 63, 83, 88, 129, 132.
Archives Photographiques, pp. 6 (b), 55, 56 (a), 57, 65 (a), 67, 68.
Alinari-Giraudon, pp. 7 (a), 159.
Haufstængl-Giraudon, p. 94.
Éditions du Seuil, pp. 6 (a), 11, 30, 109, 139, 161, 165, 170.
Roger-Viollet, pp. 56 (b), 58, 59, 65 (b), 66, 69, 74, 76, 91, 114, 142.
Bulloz, pp. 72–3.
Revue Biblique (*Gabalda*), p. 98.
Frank, p. 153.

bbi Gamaliel teaching the Torah (*Haggadah of Serajevo*)

PERIODS	RELIGIOUS EVENTS	GREAT MEN
THE AGE OF THE BIBLE		
15th or 13th cent.	The Exodus.	Moses.
	Judges and Kings.	Joshua, David, Solomon.
	The Prophets.	
	Inspired Men.	Elijah, Amos, Isaiah,
5th cent.	Completion of the Bible.	Jeremiah, Ezekiel, Ezra, Nehemiah.
THE AGE OF THE SECOND TEMPLE		
c. 444 B.C.	The Scribes. The Great Synagogue.	Simeon the Just.
	Hellenism and the Hasmonean resistance to it.	Sirach. Judas Maccabaeus.
	Jewish proselytism in the Mediterranean world: the Septuagint.	
	Spiritual trends: Sadduceeism, Essenism (the Dead Sea Scrolls), Pharisaism (teaching the Oral Law), Hellenistic philosophy, apocalyptic Messianism	The Master of Justice. Hillel. Shammai. Rabbi Gamaliel. Philo of
c. A.D. 70	(the birth of Christianity).	Alexandria. Jesus. Kephas–Peter, Saul–Paul.
THE DIASPORA: BABYLONIAN CENTRE		
c. A.D. 70	The Talmud of Jerusalem.	Rabbi Johanan ben Zakkai.
	The Talmud of Babylon.	
	The homiletical, ethical, philosophical and mystical literature of the Midrash.	Rabbi Akiba. Rabbi Judah the
	The masters of Talmudic thought: Tannaim, Amoraim, Saboraim, Gaonim	Saint. Rabbi Meir. Rab and Samuel.
9th cent.	Secession of the Karaites.	Raba and Abaye.
THE DIASPORA: WESTERN CENTRE		
9th cent.	Spain: Golden Age of theology, philosophy, poetry, mysticism.	Saadya. Solomon ibn Gabirol. Bahye.
	Beginnings of the Cabbala: the Zohar.	Judah ha Levi. Maimonides. Nahmanides.
16th cent.	France and the Rhineland:	Rashi and the Tosaphists.
	Golden Age of Biblical and Talmudical exegesis.	Gershom of Metz.
	Spiritual problems raised by persecution: messianic reconsideration of the vocation of Israel.	Meir of Rothenburg. David Reubeni. Joselmann of Rosheim.

POLITICAL EVENTS	WORLD HISTORY
Conquest of Canaan. About 1000 B.C.: Apogee of the kingdom. 586 B.C.: Fall of the first Temple. Babylonian Exile. 516 B.C.: Return and restoration.	Egypt. Phoenicia. Assyria and Chaldea. Nebuchadnezzar. The Persians: Cyrus.
165 B.C.: Revolt of the Hasmoneans. Recovery of political independence. 63 B.C.: Pompey enters Jerusalem. 40 B.C.: The reign of Herod the Great. A.D. 6.: Palestine becomes a Roman province. A.D. 67–70: War and destruction of the Second Temple.	Disintegration of the Empire of Alexander the Great. Hellenistic preponderance. The Roman Empire. Augustus, Tiberius. Vespasian, Titus.
135: Rising and defeat of the false Messiah, Bar Kocheba. 537: The edicts of Justinian: loss of civil equality and religious liberty. 641: Conversion of the Khazars to Judaism.	Hadrian. In Babylonia: the Parthian empire. Beginning of the Arab empire. Conquest of Babylonia, then of the Mediterranean (Spain).
The Crusades: massacre of the Jews. Accusations of ritual murder. 1290: Expulsion of the Jews from England. 1394: Expulsion of the Jews from France.	Hegemony of the Church in western Europe.
Gradual retreat of the Arabs in Spain. The Inquisition. 1492: Expulsion of the Jews from Spain.	Hegemony of Islam in the Mediterranean basin.

PERIODS	RELIGIOUS EVENTS	GREAT MEN
THE DIASPORA: ORIENTAL CENTRE		
16th cent.	Crystallization of Talmudic studies in Poland and Russia.	Moses Isserles.
	The mystical messianism of Safed.	Isaac Luria.
	The messianic movement of Sabbatai Zevi.	Joseph Caro.
	Popular mysticism of Hassidism in Poland.	Israel Baal Shem.
		Elias of Vilna.
		Manasse ben Israel.
18th cent.	Rationalistic and progressive renaissance in Holland, Italy and Germany.	M. H. Luzzatto.
		Moses Mendelssohn.
THE AGE OF EMANCIPATION		
	Spiritual emancipation: the Haskalah.	Nahman Krochmal.
	Assimilation.	Heinrich Heine.
	Trends: liberal, conservative, orthodox.	Abraham Geiger.
	The science of Judaism.	S. R. Hirsch.
		Leopold Zunz.
19th cent.	Doctrinal anti-semitism.	Heinrich Graetz.
	Zionism.	Theodor Herzl.
	The illusion of universal progress.	Hermann Cohen.
		Elias Benamozegh.
		Moses Montefiore.
		Aimé Pallière. Ahad Haam, H. N. Bialik, Franz Rosenzweig, Jacob Gordin.
THE THIRD REICH AND THE STATE OF ISRAEL		
20th cent.	The tragedy of solitude.	Six million martyrs.
	Human solidarity put to the test.	
	Problems of the Jewish State: the centre and the diaspora.	
	Jewish vulnerability.	
	Stocktaking.	

POLITICAL EVENTS	WORLD HISTORY
Numerous settlements in Poland and Russia. Palestine becomes a part of the Turkish empire. Development of the Dutch colony. 1657: Return of the Jews to England under Cromwell.	The Reformation.
1648: The Treaty of Westphalia attaches the Jews of Alsace to France. Massacre of Polish Jews by the Cossacks.	The Thirty Years' War.
The Age of Enlightenment brings reforms in favour of the Jews (Friedrich II, Joseph II, Louis XVI).	From absolutism to an enlightened monarchy.
1792: Emancipation of the Jews in France by a decree of the National Assembly. Emancipation of the Jews in Holland (1796) and in the other western and central European countries between 1848 and 1870. 1807: Convocation of the Great Sanhedrin by Napoleon I. 1840: The Damascus Affair.	The French Revolution. Napoleon.
1860: The Mortara Affair: Foundation of the Alliance Israélite Universelle. 1882: Beginning of systematic pogroms in Russia. 1897: The Dreyfus Affair. The first Zionist Congress at Basle. 1913: The Beilis Affair: accusation of ritual murder.	The United States of America receive immigrants.
1917: The Balfour Declaration. 1933: Hitler comes into power. 1936: The Nuremburg racial laws.	The First World War.
1939–45: The concentration camps of Auschwitz, Maidanek, Bergen-Belsen, especially intended for Jews. Liquidation of the Jews of Europe. 1941: Judaeo-Christian friendship and systems of rescue. 1943: The Warsaw Ghetto rising. 1945–48: Anti-zionist British and international policy.	The Second World War.
A tragedy reminiscent of Exodus. 1948: Proclamation of the State of Israel. 1948–9: Israel-Arab War. 1950–4: The Rosenberg Affair in the United States of America. The Slansky Affair and the Trial of the White Blouses in the Soviet sphere. Trial of Zionists in Egypt.	The Iron Curtain.

Bibliographical Notes

For the ordinary reader who wants a 'Life' of Moses the most useful single work is probably that by Sholem Asch: *Moses* (trans. Maurice Samuel: Macdonald, 1952). But there are, of course, a great many other studies, both old and recent, and a few are listed here:

FRIEDRICH VON SCHILLER, *Die Sendung Mosis* (1783).
SIEGMUND FREUD, *Moses and Monotheism* (trans. Katherine Jones: Hogarth Press, 1939).
MARTIN BUBER, *Moses* (Phaidon Press, 1946).

Mention should also be made of Thomas Mann's essay 'Moïse' in *Les Dix Commandements* (Albin Michel, 1946) and Sir Winston Churchill's delightful sketch, 'Moses, The Leader of a People', in his *Thoughts and Adventures* (Butterworth, 1932).

Many writers have seen Moses in the light of particular religious ideas. Thus Edmond Fleg's *Moïse* (Gallimard, 1928) has the background of Jewish orthodoxy. Of more ancient writers there is the first-century *Life* by Philo of Alexandria, with the background of Hellenistic Judaism, and from the fourth century the study by St Gregory of Nyssa.

In recent years many valuable contributions have been made to the history of the Jews. A useful survey is Cecil Roth's *A Short History of the Jewish People* (Macmillan, 1936). More specialized studies include those by Norman Bentwich: *Philo-Judaeus of Alexandria* (1910), *Josephus* (1914), and *Hellenism* (1919), all published by the Jewish Publication Society of America. There are also relevant passages in the *Cambridge Ancient History*, whilst Adolphe Lods' *Israel* (trans. S. H. Hooke: Kegan Paul, 1932) is also recommended. The place of the Jews in the Christian community is discussed by James Parkes in *The Conflict of the Church and the Synagogue: A Study in the Origins of Anti-Semitism* (1934) and *The Jew in the Medieval Community* (1938); both published by the Soncino Press. Zionism is the subject of Israel Cohen's *The Zionist Movement* (Muller, 1945), and also, to a large extent, of *Trial and Error* (Hamish Hamilton, 1949), the autobiography of Chaïm Weitzmann, first President of modern Israel.

The intellectual and artistic influence of Judaism is successfully discussed in *The Legacy of Israel* (Oxford University Press, 1927) by I. Abrahams, E. Bevan and C. Singer. Also recommended are: Cecil Roth, *The Jewish Contribution to Civilisation* (Macmillan, 1938) and Meyer Waxman, *A History of Jewish Literature* (4 vols., New York, 1930–41).

The archaeological and theological problems inherent in Old Testament study are examined, and the findings of recent research made available, in *The Old Testament and Modern Study: A Generation of Discovery and Research* (Oxford, 1951), a symposium edited by H. H. Rowley and published by The Society for Old Testament Study.

It must be admitted, however, that the true heart, the spirituality, of Israel, and therefore of the significance and vitality of Moses, is missing from all the books we have so far mentioned; for it is something that can only be derived from a study of the actual sources of Jewish spirituality. Such a study is not easily accessible to the English reader both because very little is available in English translation and because the original Hebrew is itself a language which is hardly susceptible to translation. True, there is now available the excellent French *Jerusalem Bible*[1] (Editions du Cerf), of which the Old Testament is scrupulously based on the Hebrew originals, and there are English versions of the Talmud and of certain important rabbinical commentaries (especially the *Mishneh Torah* and the *Guide of the Perplexed* of the twelfth-century rabbi Moses Maimonides), but all these should be studied in Hebrew if they are to reveal their full significance: and to them should be added the *Zohar* or *Book of Splendour*, a mystical commentary in Aramaic upon the Pentateuch; and the more important writings of Rashi (Rabbi Solomon ben Isaac of Troyes: 1040–1105), Judah ha Levi (1075–1141) and Joseph Caro (1488–1575). Above all, the Bible should be read in the original Hebrew, the language of its authors and now once more of the ordinary people of the Holy Land.

Finally, two excellent books in which contemporary Jewish thought is expounded:

F. Rosenzweig, *Der Stern der Erlösung* (Schocken, 1920), and
A. Heschel, *God in Search of Man* (The Jewish Publication Society of America: Philadelphia, 1956).

[1] An English edition is being prepared by the Rev. Alex. Jones, for publication in England by Messrs. Longmans, Green and Co., and in the U.S.A. by Messrs. Doubleday, Doubleday and Co.

LONGMANS, GREEN AND CO LTD
6 & 7 CLIFFORD STREET, LONDON W1
THIBAULT HOUSE, THIBAULT SQUARE, CAPE TOWN
605–611 LONSDALE STREET, MELBOURNE C1
443 LOCKHART ROAD, HONG KONG
ACCRA, AUCKLAND, IBADAN
KINGSTON (JAMAICA), KUALA LUMPUR
LAHORE, NAIROBI, SALISBURY (RHODESIA)
LONGMANS, GREEN AND CO INC
119 WEST 40TH STREET, NEW YORK 18
LONGMANS, GREEN AND CO
20 CRANFIELD ROAD, TORONTO 16
ORIENT LONGMANS PRIVATE LTD
CALCUTTA, BOMBAY, MADRAS
DELHI, HYDERABAD, DACCA

HARPER AND BROTHERS
49 EAST 33RD STREET
NEW YORK 16

First published in France
by Editions du Seuil, Paris

This English edition first published 1959

Library of Congress Catalog Card Number 59–6652

TYPE SET BY WESTERN PRINTING SERVICES LTD., BRISTOL
PRINTED IN GREAT BRITAIN BY LOWE AND BRYDONE (PRINTERS) LTD.